Totalitarianism
and American Social Thought

Robert Allen Skotheim
University of Colorado

HOLT, RINEHART AND WINSTON, INC.

New York   Chicago   San Francisco   Atlanta
Dallas   Montreal   Toronto   London   Sydney

To Thomas J. Pressly,
who first suggested to me the significance of the history of the idea of totalitarianism in modern American social thought

Copyright © 1971 by Holt, Rinehart and Winston, Inc.
All Rights Reserved
Library of Congress Catalog Card Number: 77–169615
ISBN: 0–03–084402–9
Printed in the United States of America
1 2 3 4   090   9 8 7 6 5 4 3 2 1

Foreword

The study of history is an absorbing and complex matter. Historians, whether they act as teachers or writers or both, are engaged in several interrelated tasks—discovery, interpretation, reinterpretation, and synthesis. Specialists who have discovered new data often have difficulty communicating it; their findings often reach the public third- or fourth-hand. Sometimes discovery comes in the interpretation or reinterpretation of known facts; even here "middle men" are often the ones who reach the public.

The Berkshire Studies in American History are designed to bring to a wide audience a variety of works by professional historians. Contrary to some popular impressions, there are many genuine historians who know how to write for a wide public. This series is an outlet for them. Each book in it is devoted to an important theme closely related to the author's main scholarly interests.

Robert Allen Skotheim has written an account of the impact of the concept of totalitarianism on the thinking of American intellectuals. While his focus is on the ramifications of the idea of totalitarianism, he also describes and analyzes the nature of pragmatic and progressive thought, the system which an awareness of totalitarianism came to affect. His own method is biographical and selective; it has the very great advantage of being at the same time human and specific. The reader of this original and provocative book can follow the developing social thought of some very interesting people, and he can also watch while Skotheim dissects them.

Robert E. Burke, Series Editor
Berkshire Studies in American History

Preface

American historians have become increasingly concerned during the last several decades with the role of mind or thought in human affairs. As the specialty of intellectual history, or history of ideas, has developed, every field of historical study has paid more attention to intellectual factors. It is no longer fashionable among leading historians to dismiss men's thoughts as mere reflections or reflexes of an external reality. That the perception of reality is itself a subjective act, that what men do is influenced by what they think they can do and ought to do, that even so-called inanimate forces such as economic developments occur through the agency of human beings, are propositions increasingly acknowledged by historians.

Even though it is true that scholars are emphasizing the intellectual factor in history, this does not mean that they agree precisely as to how it should be emphasized, or that those specializing in the history of ideas all write the same kind of intellectual history. Some scholars dwell upon the ideas of an intellectual elite, while others examine more popular beliefs. Some investigate the internal structure or composition of ideas, while others highlight the relation between thought and behavior. Some study social thought, or ideas concerning society, while others analyze more philosophical or "cultural" or esthetic themes. Some try to locate climates of opinion, or the spirit of the age, while others pursue the history of particular ideas.

The broad concern of this book is with the changing climates of opinion in the United States between the early 1900s and the 1970s. From the turn of the century into the Great Depression, there was a reform spirit of great strength. This reform mood gave way during the 1940s and 1950s to a more conservative intellectual temper. The 1960s saw the emergence, particularly on the part of a young generation, of a new preoccupation with reform and radicalism which challenged the conservatism as well as the milder liberalism of older generations.

More narrowly, I have presented certain assumptions, methods, and value judgments in the social thought of some of the intellectuals who expressed characteristics of the changing climates of opinion. More specifically still, I have tried to indicate the relevance of what I call the idea, or the changing ideas, of totalitarianism to these assumptions, methods, and value judgments. At times the idea of totalitarianism, which will be defined in the course of the study, seems to act as a creative intellectual force, changing men's minds and influencing the climate of opinion at large. On other occasions the idea of totalitarianism appears instead merely to reflect more general patterns of ideas. In either case it has been integral to the history of modern American social thought.

The rather sweeping historical generalizations I have offered concerning social thought are supported by a necessarily rigid selection of people and ideas discussed. The aim is not comprehensiveness, even for a particular period in the past. The goal is rather to indicate the changing and continuous outlines of patterns of thought by an examination of selected themes. So, for example, the penultimate chapter on the radicalism of the 1960s is not an attempt to explore the admitted complexity and variety of the rapidly changing radical phenomenon, but instead to suggest the historical dimension of certain aspects of contemporary radicalism. Different readers will disagree as to whether these selected aspects express the center or the periphery, the best or the worst, of radical thought.

I would add a word concerning the frequent reference to "intellectuals." There is a lack of agreement as to what precisely is meant by the term, but American historians continue to use it in lieu of a better alternative. Admitting that there is no rigidly defined intellectual class in the United States, historians nevertheless frequently refer to men of letters, political thinkers, scholars, artists, and journalists as intellectuals. Most often the term is used merely as a convenience to allude to those individuals who express themselves at greatest length on matters of interest to the historians. Usually this means those who engage in social criticism. It is in this general way that I use the term. I do not include within my definition any necessary alienation or estrangement from society on the part of the intellectual, although part of the story to be told concerns the estrangement of some of the intellectuals.

For those readers who would explore further the ideas and the people presented here, as well as their times and intellectual contemporaries, I have included Suggestions for Further Reading. Wherever they are available, I have indicated paperback editions of the works suggested.

I would like to thank the Graduate School of Wayne State University (Detroit, Michigan) and the John Simon Guggenheim Memorial Foundation for fellowships which at different times relieved me from teaching responsibilities so that I could do research in the history of the American reaction to European totalitarianism. I am at present engaged in various studies resulting from these researches.

Robert Allen Skotheim

Boulder, Colorado
July 1971

Contents

Foreword   iii
Preface   v

1. AN OVERVIEW   *1*

2. PRAGMATIC AND PROGRESSIVE SOCIAL THOUGHT
   IN THE EARLY 1900s: ASSUMPTIONS AND METHODS   *12*

   Change, Progress, and the Problem of Values:
   James Harvey Robinson (1863–1936)   *15*

   Change, Disillusionment, and Progress:
   Walter Lippmann, I (1899–   )   *19*

   Pragmatism and Progressive Values: William James (1842–1910)
   and John Dewey (1859–1952)   *23*

   Sympathetic Pragmatic and Progressive Interpretations of European Dictatorships in the 1920s: William Henry Chamberlin, I (1897–1969)
   and Lincoln Steffens (1866–1936)   *29*

3. THE DISCOVERY OF EUROPEAN TOTALITARIANISM
   IN THE 1930s   *38*

   The Dictatorial Dream That Failed: William Henry Chamberlin, II   *40*

Marxism as Pragmatism and Theology: Sidney Hook, I (1902–   ) *44*

Old and Outworn Values Become New and Relevant:
  Walter Lippmann, II *52*

Culture and Commitment: Joseph Wood Krutch (1893–1970) *59*

4. PROGRESSIVISM IN ECLIPSE: A NEW CONSERVATISM
   IN THE 1940s AND 1950s *68*

Isolationist to Cold Warrior: William Henry Chamberlin, III *70*

Liberty and Authority in an Age of Totalitarianism: Sidney Hook, II *75*

Absolutism and Practicality: Walter Lippmann, III *82*

Stability, Retrogression, and the Problem of Values:
  Richard Hofstadter (1916–1970) *87*

5. A NEW RADICALISM, A NEW BOHEMIANISM, AND
   A NEW IDEA OF TOTALITARIANISM IN THE 1960s *94*

From the Old Left to the New: C. Wright Mills (1916–1962) *96*

The Radical Politics of History: Howard Zinn (1922–   ) *106*

Life-Style and the Revolution: James Simon Kunen (1948–   ) *112*

6. AN ASSESSMENT *120*

Suggestions for Further Reading 125
Index 131

1

AN OVERVIEW[1]

A great deal of the history of modern American social thought can be told in terms of the discovery, development, and rejection of ideas of totalitarianism. The first widespread "discovery of totalitarianism" in the 1930s accompanied the transformation from the earlier twentieth-century progressive and pragmatic climate of opinion to the more conservative intellectual temper that became dominant during the 1940s and 1950s. The first totalitarianism to be discovered was European in origin, and was found in Mussolini's Italy, Hitler's Germany, and Stalin's Russia. Americans who interpreted the idea of totalitarianism argued that Italian, German, and Russian societies sacrificed the individual human personality for the purposes of the State. As these Americans located the existence of totalitarianism in Europe, they simultaneously rallied to the defense of Ameri-

---

[1] This overview essay was first given as a public lecture at the University of Denver on May 5, 1969. Later it appeared in the *Denver Quarterly* 4 (Winter 1970):19–33, under the title "American 'Discoveries of Totalitarianism' in the Twentieth Century," from which it is reprinted, with some minor revision, by permission of that journal.

can society and its democratic constitutional system. The role of the United States, both in World War II and the Cold War, was supported in the name of resistance to Fascist totalitarianism during the Cold War. Domestic American conditions throughout the 1940s and 1950s were defended by the same Americans who identified the idea of totalitarianism in Europe on the grounds that, in comparison with totalitarian societies, conditions in the United States were basically humane, and conducive to the liberty of the individual—however imperfect if judged by an ideal standard. Throughout the 1960s and 1970s this has remained the perspective of most Americans born prior to the Great Depression. Among the younger generations born during and after the 1930s there are many who reject or are indifferent to their elders' earlier perceptions of totalitarianism in Europe, and consequent celebration of the existing order in America. These young radicals have made during the 1960s and 1970s a second discovery of totalitarianism, this time arguing that it is located in the government and society of the United States. Estrangement from, and rebellion against, traditional American institutions have accompanied the younger generations' development of the new idea of totalitarianism in the United States. As the young confront the old in what is, among other things, the most serious generational conflict in American history, the contrasting ideas of totalitarianism are explicitly and implicitly at issue. While a historical review of the ideas cannot by itself answer the question of who today is right and who is wrong, a history of the ideas can perhaps provide a more informed and sympathetic understanding of the present conflict in social thought.

The years prior to World War I witnessed the same blend of hope and experimentation in American social thought as is seen in today's young radicals. Early twentieth-century reformers were self-consciously progressive and pragmatic. What the progressives argued was basically wrong with existing institutions, ideas, and habits was that they were relics of an earlier historical period. What was wrong was that men held on to old ways after a new environment had come into existence. Progressives concluded that every new environment needed new policies to accompany it, because the old policies were bound to be irrelevant. It was, for example, irrelevant to carry over traditional legal concepts of negligence, formed in agricultural environments, after complex and dangerous machinery came into use in an industrial environment. To compel the injured worker to bear the financial burden of accidents unless he could demonstrate in court that someone else was negligent, the reformers argued, was to ignore the new and real conditions of life. Similarly, in an industrial environment of working conditions injurious to health after long hours of exposure, progressives argued that it was irrelevant to speak of the legitimacy of traditional rights of contract which allowed a worker to bind himself to work any number of hours. New environments required new principles. What was progressive about this approach was that the reformers assumed that the new principles would be better than the ones to be replaced.

The importance of an experimental method to this approach was obvious. Up-to-date hypotheses, policies, or answers had to be investigated, and outworn ones had to be discarded. The pragmatic or instrumental method of William James and John Dewey answered the needs of the progressive reformer. The pragmatic method, James explained, helped to eliminate from consideration beliefs and policies which were irrelevant to the present situation. The pragmatic method was a way of discussing or analyzing alternative hypotheses and principles in terms of their practical consequences in specific situations. If such-and-such a belief were acted upon, if this or that policy were adopted, what would be the consequences? After the various alternatives were examined in terms of their practical results, the pragmatic method would have served its purpose—to compel analysis along pragmatic lines. The reformers' assumption was that when value judgment decisions were made concerning the adoption of one policy or solution as against another, its adoption would be on the pragmatic grounds of its ability to cope with specific present problems. Forever banished, progressives hoped, would be the nonpragmatic appeal to traditional absolutist, outworn principles, policies, or beliefs which had nothing to do with the present environment and today's problems.

Prior to World War I, progressive and pragmatic reformers in the United States took for granted that significant social improvement could and would occur within the fabric of America's democratic constitutional system. Reformers did not have to face the question of whether they would defend attempted change outside the system. But in their disillusionment after World War I, together with their realization that not only were the prewar reforms of limited significance but that most of the American people were not interested in reform at all in the postwar years, some Americans adopted a radical stance for the first time. A few during the 1920s, and a great number in the 1930s, decided that society's problems could be solved only by a radical and total reconstruction of the social order. Though radicalism between the two world wars constituted an escalation of prewar liberalism, the later radical stance worked almost completely from the intellectual base of prewar progressive and pragmatic thought.

America's interwar radicals developed a rationale in defense of revolution which was strikingly similar to today's young radicals' justification for the use of violence. Since in the 1920s radical change was not occurring in the United States, European revolutionary governments became the focus of attention for Americans contemplating the wisdom of revolutionary change. From those who were sympathetic to the European dictatorships, there emerged a progressive and pragmatic defense of dictatorial experimentation. The defense was pragmatic insofar as it argued that the dictatorship should be allowed to work itself out in order to determine its practical consequences. It was a progressive defense insofar as it optimistically equated revolutionary change with betterment.

The Soviet Union received the most consistent progressive and pragmatic defense from sympathetic Americans throughout the 1920s and 1930s. Russia was regarded as a laboratory for social experiment, in which mankind was testing hypotheses. As when observing a scientific experiment, so when watching the Soviet Union, it was necessary to postpone judgment until the experiment was over, and then to judge its success in terms of its own goals. This adoption of an implicit relativism allowed admirers of Russian revolutionary dictatorship to admit that State suppression of dissenting opinion was not what Americans had traditionally regarded as the best practice, but to insist at the same time that traditional American ideals were irrelevant to the Soviet Union. Because American constitutional and legal provisions that protected individuals and minorities also, and more fundamentally, protected the capitalistic status quo, the radicals argued, the purpose of the American system was completely different from that of the Soviet dictatorship, which was the destruction of capitalism and the establishment of proletarian rule. Liberty in the Soviet Union meant something different from what it meant in the United States, and the proper pragmatic question to ask was what were the practical consequences of the different conceptions. The Left radicals suggested that the practical consequences of the American conception might be shown to be a narrow political and civil liberty for everyone, but a broad economic and social liberty for only the favored few; whereas the practical consequences of the Communist conception might turn out to be a broad economic and social liberty for everyone, which would thereby render meaningless the admitted lack of political and civil liberty as understood by Americans. The radicals further argued that revolutionary violence would in any case not be necessary as soon as the Bolshevik experiment was secure. It was temporarily necessary to use violent means in order to achieve good ends. When critics objected that bad means had a way of corrupting noble ends, the Left responded that immediate and harsh judgments against dictatorial experimentation in the Soviet Union revealed an unfortunate and inflexible moral absolutism and a lack of sophisticated understanding of the experimental method. This pragmatic and progressive defense of revolutionary change was invoked only by those who were critical of American society and who were sympathetic with the avowed aims of the revolutionary dictatorship. As for the young radicals of the 1960s, so for the old interwar radicals, good goals brought a justification for violence.

The last time around, in the 1930s, the radical argument that the ends justified the means was undermined by the first discovery of totalitarianism. The development of the idea of totalitarianism during the Depression decade accompanied the destruction of the progressive and pragmatic justification of revolutionary change. There came a point for most of the old radicals when Soviet purges, trials, and executions seemed to be not merely unfortunate but necessary means to desirable ends, but instead evil means which rendered the avowed ends irrelevant. There came a point for most of the Left in the later 1930s when it seemed that the Soviet Union was no different from the Fascist dictatorships in its ruthless subjugation of the individual. The location of European societies and governments which, irrespective of their declared goals, ignored civil liberties, suppressed minorities, and eroded the autonomy of the human personality, constituted the first American discovery of totalitarianism.

The word "totalitarian" was an anglicization of the Italian word which the Fascists coined in the 1920s to describe Mussolini's system, and the earliest explicit preoccupation with totalitarianism in the 1930s concerned Germany and Italy. The significance of the common early definition of totalitarianism in terms of fascism rather than of communism, of Germany and Italy instead of Russia, was that it allowed those Americans who sympathized with the Soviet Union to continue their progressive and pragmatic defense of the Bolshevik experiment. As long as totalitarianism was applied only to Fascists, and not also to Communists, it did not alter the view of political and social reality which was familiar to the radical and to the liberal reformer. Communism in the Soviet Union could still be viewed as Left, which meant progressive, irrespective of the means used to achieve forward-looking ends. Fascism in Germany could still be viewed as Right, which meant reactionary. Left and Right retained their utility as the decisive standards.

But increasingly during the later 1930s the idea of totalitarianism was defined in terms common to fascism and communism, in terms common to the Soviet Union as well as to Germany and Italy. Increasingly, it was argued that the psychology, coercion, and ultimate tyranny of the Left was much the same as that of the Right. In an identical way the individual gave up his life to the community consciousness of the State. The Soviet purge trials between 1936–1938 accelerated the American interpretation of totalitarianism in which the Russians shared. By the spring of 1939 a group of well-known intellectuals, including John Dewey, Sidney Hook, Horace Kallen, Ferdinand Lundberg, and Eugene Lyons, organized the Committee for Cultural Freedom explicitly in order to enunciate the idea that totalitarianism was on the Left as well as on the Right. "Under varying labels and colors, but with an unvarying hatred for the free mind, the totalitarian idea is already enthroned in Germany, Italy, Russia, Japan and Spain," the Committee's statement read in May of 1939, centrally placing the Soviet Union in the middle of four Fascist dictatorships. Other signatories to the statement of the Committee for Cultural Freedom included Sherwood Anderson, Carl Becker, V. F. Calverton, Elmer Davis, Max Eastman, Sinclair Lewis, John Dos Passos, Norman Thomas, and Oswald Garrison Villard. "Art, science, and education" in totalitarian countries, the statement continued, "have been forcibly turned into lackeys for a supreme state, a deified leader and an official pseudo-philosophy."[2] A large group of intellectuals who remained sympathetic to the Soviet Union in the spring of 1939, including Waldo Frank, Granville Hicks, Matthew Josephson, Corliss Lamont, Max Lerner, Clifford Odets, Frederick Schuman, Vincent Sheean, I. F. Stone, Louis Untermeyer, James Thurber, and William Carlos Williams, felt that the Committee for Cultural Freedom was incorrectly defining totalitarianism to include the Russians. In an open letter of protest, they argued that all men of good will should be unified against fascism, and that the unified front was undermined when the Committee for Cultural Freedom "encouraged the fantastic falsehood that the U.S.S.R. and the totalitarian states are basically alike."[3] The open protest letter was published first in *The Daily Worker*, and then reprinted in *The Nation*. Unfortunately for the group, their public argument for the irreconcilable opposition of Russian communism and German fascism appeared in the same issue of *The Nation* on August 26 that carried the news of the Nazi-Soviet nonaggression pact. Hitler and Stalin publicly agreed to live at peace with each other, and privately agreed to dismember Poland between them. The Nazi-Soviet pact significantly contributed to the first interpretation of totalitarianism as a concept that linked the revolutionary dictatorships of both Right and Left.

Americans who already by August of 1939 had banished the Communists to the same category of dictatorships as that of the Fascists were confirmed in their views with the revelation of the Nazi-Soviet pact. Most Americans who prior to August remained pro-Soviet were disillusioned by the pact and began for the first time to include the Russians in their definition of totalitarianism. It is perhaps a measure of the utopianism of radical thought between the two world wars that the nonaggression agreement should have so demoralized those who had up to that point continued to keep the faith. Why were so few of the Americans who had

---

[2] Quoted by Eugene Lyons, *The Red Decade* (Indianapolis: Bobbs-Merrill, 1941), p. 344.

[3] Lyons, *The Red Decade*, p. 347. The exact phrasing of the sentence is taken from *The Nation* 149 (August 26, 1939):228.

previously argued that the Soviets were the beacon light of world progress able to defend Soviet foreign policy on grounds of national security? If Russian survival were necessary for progress, and if an imminent German invasion could not be repelled in 1939, then a realistic analysis might sympathize with Stalin's attempt to stall while he prepared a military defense. But the view of most Americans sympathetic to the Soviets was much too ideological and even millennial for such a realistic analysis, despite their seemingly hardheaded defense of Communist experimentation during the 1920s and 1930s. The same utopianism which earlier placed Communist dictatorship on the side of the angels in a holy war, after August of 1939 tended to reject the Soviets absolutely as totalitarians.

America was embraced by its intellectuals in direct proportion to the discovery of totalitarianism in the European revolutionary dictatorships and the consequent lumping of Stalin's Russia with Hitler's Germany and Mussolini's Italy. Antagonism on the part of many intellectuals toward the American status quo, a hostility which went back in some cases to the years around World War I, was increasingly dispelled as the European alternatives were judged worse and worse. Students of literature are familiar with the reembracement of America which was manifested in the works of so many writers during and after the late 1930s. Sinclair Lewis, muckraker of the Babbitts on Main Street in the 1920s, revealed a concern for the preservation of traditional America when he warned in *It Can't Happen Here* (1935) of the possibility of a totalitarian (Fascist primarily, but Lewis explicitly stated in the novel that the Communists were no better) seizure of power in the United States. John Dos Passos, unusual among America's writers in the 1920s for his political preoccupations, turned away from two decades of radicalism with a tribute to American history appreciatively called *The Ground We Stand On* (1941). Historians participated as much as did literary figures in the reembracement of America. A warmer and more sympathetic view of the history of the United States, an interpretation which was inclined to praise American ideas and institutions rather than to criticize them and to indicate the need for reform, became increasingly common in historical scholarship. Charles Beard, the author before World War I of a famous economic interpretation of the United States Constitution which implicitly emphasized its limitations and the need to change it, came in the era of European totalitarianism and of American reembracement to celebrate what he called the perennially great features of the Constitution. Having written before World War I that all public rules were simply mirrors of the dominant power interests in society, Beard wrote in the 1930s that democratic constitutional procedure was to be valued as the guarantee of human liberty. Carl Becker, who in the 1920s argued in a book on the ideas of the Declaration of Independence that they were neither true nor false but merely pragmatically useful or useless at any particular time, reissued the book in 1941 with a new preface in which he spoke of the eternal truth of Jeffersonian Enlightenment thought. Such examples suggest the intellectual dimensions of the reembracement of America following the discovery of totalitarianism in Europe.

The implications of the first American discovery of European totalitarianism exceeded literary and historical reembracement. They became in effect the rationale for American participation in World War II and the Cold War, and for the lack of more extensive domestic reform throughout the last quarter-century. The rationale for foreign policy, quite apart from considerations of national security, was that America was the bastion of freedom in a world threatened by aggressive totalitarians. The rationale for domestic politics was that the existing American social order was basically sound.

The older generations which grew into intellectual and political leadership in the United States during and after the late 1940s were born before or around World War I. Whatever may previously have been their criticisms of America and their hopes for change, in the years following World War II they were by and large defenders of the existent system. This conservative face of the older generations was the only face their children saw by the 1960s. The young activists as well as those who merely withdrew, the New Left and the "hippies," saw in their parents an acceptance of perpetual war abroad and racism and poverty at home. Their parents' idea of totalitarianism as a characteristic of utopian revolutionaries who sacrificed life and human dignity in the exercise of dictatorship no longer was persuasive to younger generations of Americans. From the perspective of the 1960s the Soviet Union had liberalized, Franco had softened, fascism was otherwise gone from Europe, and international communism had split into factions. Not only did young radicals reject the older interpretation of European totalitarianism but they made a second and different "discovery of totalitarianism."

In their new interpretation the New Left located totalitarianism in the government and society of the United States. The young radicals argued that America was guilty of depressing its poor and racial minorities, of dehumanizing its affluent citizens, and of forcing its will and military power upon defenseless peoples around the world. The New Left argued that an imperialistic foreign policy of continual war was necessary to keep the American economy prosperous. The young radicals contended that the older generations prosecuted antirevolutionary foreign interventions without moral examination of the violent means to effect antirevolutionary Cold War ends. They further argued that domestically the United States was not a genuinely open society, but rather a closed economic and racial corporation preoccupied with maintaining its own power.

It was a measure of the New Left's perception of the legitimacy of the word and idea of totalitarianism to Americans that the young radicals in the 1960s came to create their own definition of totalitarianism in the course of their attack on the established order. So influential had been the older interpretation of European totalitarianism, the New Left thought, and so conservative had been its implications, that the New Left developed the idea that America was itself totalitarian. Hoping to cancel out the specter of a foreign revolutionary dictatorship which would drive Americans to an uncritical defense of things-as-they-are in the United States, the young radicals' concept of America as a totalitarian society would instead demand an attack on the status quo.

The New Left's increasing argument, as the 1960s moved into the 1970s, that American society was totalitarian, coincided with the increasing militancy of the young radicals. Just as the Old Left defended revolutionary violence in the European dictatorships on the grounds of the hopeless degradation of the old order, so the New Left came by the late 1960s and early 1970s to justify violence in the United States through the argument that the established order was totalitarian. Paralleling the rationale of the Old Left, the New Left said that when social conditions get bad enough, the "dispossessed" poor and minorities are systematically violated by the established order. Since the peaceful procedures of the society have been turned into institutions of oppression, they have lost their ability to command loyalty. The radical use of violence is thus different in name only from the legal violence sanctioned by society. Further reminiscent of the stance of the interwar radicals, the New Left foresaw the same progressive possibility of utopia. Escalating violence, deprivation of democratic constitutional process and civil liberties, and disruption of the social order were ultimately justified as a transition to a better future society. As for the Old Left, so for the New Left, admittedly bad means were defended by the invocation of noble goals.

At this point a scholarly survey of the ideas of totalitarianism must draw solely upon today's name-calling polemics. The older generations are simultaneously appalled and saddened to see the young radicals repeating the Old Left's "ends justify the means" rationale for violence. The New Left is simultaneously embittered and stimulated by the failure of the older generations to see that the young radicals are the hope of America.

It is clear that the older generations, including the Old Left, have lost their legitimacy for the young radicals. The reembracement of America by the old radicals in the 1930s following their discovery of totalitarianism was so complete, their post-World War II support of an ideological war was so uncompromising, their disinclination to probe into America's failing was so marked, that the New Left can perhaps be excused for its otherwise apparently arrogant contention that it is the first generation in history to understand and to criticize life in the United States.

It is equally clear that today's young radicals appear largely ignorant of the extent to which they have repeated the Old Left's defense of violence, and insofar as they are aware of the parallel they seem insensitive to the inherent moral problems attached to it. Like the old radicals, the New Left couples its severe indictment of present conditions with utopian hopes for the future. As Daniel Bell, a disillusioned Old Leftist, recently wrote in criticism of the young radicals:

> Coming "out of themselves," with no sense of the past, they have a callow vitality, drive, and hubris, uncomplicated by notions of history, complexity, tragedy, or doubt. And yet, though they reject the radicals of the 1930s, the New Leftists are like them in an uncanny way . . . secure in their belief that they were on the express train of History, [the old radicals] were equally heedless of the few small voices that warned them of the wreckages of the past and of those that might lie ahead. (When told of Kronstadt, the episode in 1921 when Lenin and Trotsky shot down the revolutionary Red sailors because they were demanding free elections, the young communists of the Thirties would say, jeeringly, "Who cares about old history?")[4]

The question of course is whether the implicit historical determinism in Bell's statement is justified. The New Left, as a dissident minority protesting the established order, is already guilty of defending violence in the name of the good cause. But would the young radicals defend a dictatorial totalitarianism in power? The New Left's indifference to civil liberties, impatience with democratic constitutionalism, intolerance toward differences of opinion, and hostility to traditional scholarly inquiry and detachment, are not encouraging. The young radicals themselves deny that they will become thoroughgoing totalitarians. They insist that this time around revolutionary tactics can bring a freer society. Since he cannot foresee the future, the historian cannot deny this possibility. It must be admitted that the future is at least partly open. But, as Daniel Bell concludes, in *Marxian Socialism in the United States*:

---

[4] Daniel Bell, *Marxian Socialism in the United States* (Princeton, N. J.: Princeton University Press, 1967), p. xii.

While it is too facile to say that a generation which does not know its own past is bound to repeat those errors, it is possible that a generation which knows its past is more likely to make more intelligent decisions about its future. And that is the virtue of History.[5]

---

[5] Bell, *Marxian Socialism*, p. xii.

2

PRAGMATIC AND PROGRESSIVE
SOCIAL THOUGHT IN THE EARLY 1900s
Assumptions and Methods

The years following the Civil War brought new conditions
of life to Americans. Increasing consolidation of capital,
labor, production, and distribution occurred as industrialization proceeded. Accompanying economic consolidation
was the migration of people to the cities from Europe and
from rural America. New York City's growth from roughly
one and one-half million in 1870 to approximately three and
one-half million at the turn of the century illustrated one
aspect of the change, and the increase in railroad trackage
from about 40,000 miles in 1860 to nearly 200,000 in 1900
showed another. The application of modern science and
technology resulted in the appearance of the new steel and
oil industries which elevated Andrew Carnegie and John D.
Rockefeller to the pantheon of organizational giants. Historians now speak, in the phrase of Professor Robert Wiebe,
of a national "search for order" after the Civil War, as
small and almost autonomous units of life in a rural society
passed into the increasingly interdependent, ordered, technological world of the urbanized twentieth century.

 The new environmental conditions in the late nineteenth century accompanied tenaciously held moral traditions which had not basically changed for generations. Among these the most important for the history of social thought was widespread belief in the ability of every individual to improve his worldly position through hard work. Called the Self-Help myth by historians, its origins were theological. Seventeenth-century Puritans articulated the doctrine of a double calling, by which it was stipulated that each man was to pursue a particular calling by making a success of his vocation in this world as well as a more general calling in the service of the Lord in an attempt to achieve salvation in the next world. By the turn of the eighteenth century the venerable Puritan Cotton Mather was willing to give particular emphasis to the material rewards of disciplined hard work. "A Christian should follow his occupation with industry," he wrote. "A diligent man is very rarely an indigent man. Would a man rise by his business? I say, then let him rise to his business," answered Mather. "Young man, work hard while you are young, and you'll reap the effects of it, when you are old."[1] The young Benjamin Franklin read Cotton Mather, and in his own writings later in the eighteenth century dropped the general calling in quest of other worldly salvation, but otherwise he merely elaborated on Mather's method for success in this world. Franklin gave detailed advice concerning punctuality, frugality, honesty, loyalty, temperance, moderation, cleanliness, humility, and other virtues which were simultaneously of practical and moral worth. Franklin's secularized advice was repeated throughout the nineteenth century as bountiful economic opportunity appeared to respond to many Americans who heeded the dictates of hard work.

Franklin and his Self-Help followers were not merely providing a handbook for making money. They were offering a general moral philosophy with specific implications for public policy. In general, the Self-Help myth portrayed a moral world of self-reliant individuals making their own destinies. Because the world was righteously ordered, Franklin's virtues were effective tools for success. It followed that because of the moral order, sloth as well as dishonesty would bring failure. More specifically, in terms of public policy, the Self-Help myth implied the wisdom of a negative hands-off governmental stance toward economic and social relations in the society. Since deserving men were able to make their own way in a moral world, there was no reason for government to intervene—particularly on the side of the weak, the poor, and the disabled. Never eroded altogether as an article of belief among Americans, the Self-Help dogma has been called especially influential during the late nineteenth century as an intellectual factor that contributed to the maintenance of the status quo.

---

[1] Quoted in Michael McGiffert, ed. *Puritanism and the American Experience* (Reading, Mass.: Addison-Wesley, 1969), p. 124. (Punctuation altered.)

Historians also emphasize another idea, or cluster of ideas, which helped undermine reform in the late nineteenth century. Less popular among the population at large and more the property of the intellectuals who admired Charles Darwin's evolutionary theory, Conservative Social Darwinism was a translation from biological science to social policy. Darwin, in *The Origin of Species* (1859), argued that evolution occurred through a "natural selection" process by which those individual organisms most able to cope with their environment transmitted by heredity their superior characteristics. While those incapable of adapting to the environment failed to perpetuate themselves, those most fit ultimately created new species which carried evolution forward. It was no doubt predictable that a transfer of Darwin's ideas to contemporary society would occur among some social thinkers who took their own high position in the world to be evidence that they had been naturally selected to lead the human race. Conservative Social Darwinists argued that mankind had progressed to its present civilization through a process of the "survival of the fittest." Struggle between and among individuals was accented; strong individuals had perpetuated themselves and thus, in the long run, lifted up the entire human race. This jungle metaphor of tooth and claw struggle reinforced the contemporary political implications of the Self-Help doctrine insofar as Conservative Social Darwinism also theoretically discouraged community aid to the unfit as foolish sentimentalism.

As the nineteenth century drew to a close, however, criticisms of the Self-Help myth and Conservative Social Darwinism mounted. Critics increasingly denied that the self-reliance formula of Benjamin Franklin was an adequate guide to life in an urban, industrial society. They insisted that Conservative Social Darwinists did not accurately indicate how man had progressed. The counterargument of critics, called Reform Darwinian by historians, said that man had progressed not through competitive jungle struggle but instead through intelligent, planned cooperation in dealing with his environment. The complex environment of modern society therefore required unprecedented group analysis and action. Admitting the influence of the environment in shaping its inhabitants, Reform Darwinists declared that human beings also had the power to reshape the environment and thus to reshape themselves. The implications for public policy were the reverse of the rags-to-riches myth and Conservative Social Darwinism. Reform Darwinism implicitly challenged the status quo and asked if the social order might not be better rearranged.

During the 1880s and 1890s such ideas slowly penetrated the thinking of American intellectuals, and exploded in a burst of reform activity which marked virtually all areas of life by the time the United States entered World War I. Sociological legal theorists Oliver Wendell Holmes, Roscoe Pound, and Louis Brandeis led an attempt to make the law more responsive to a changing society. Organized religion expressed a commitment to public reform in the social gospel movement led by Protestants who wanted to make Christianity relevant to industrial life. John Dewey's progressive educational reforms tried to involve the child more fully in the learning process, and the school more completely in the social process. The list of reform activities is long and varied. The name "progressive" is attached to the reformers because of their conviction that the changes constituted progress. Progressivism in politics resulted when demands for political and economic change percolated upward from the cities to state governments and finally to Congress and to the presidency. By the election of 1912 three of the four presidential candidates, Democratic winner Woodrow Wilson, Progressive ex-President Theodore Roosevelt, and Socialist Eugene Debs, who all together polled more than three-fourths of the total vote, ran as reformers, and even the conservative, President William Howard Taft, agreed with much of progressivism—or at least said he did. Because the progressive reform mentality was so pervasive in the early 1900s, historians refer to an overall progressive climate of opinion, or a progressive spirit of the age.

Because progressive social thought, like any body of ideas concerning society, comprised an intellectual strategy for dealing with certain conditions, it is important to ask whether the strategy did what it was supposed to do. In other words, did progressive thought help reform society in the early twentieth century? But that question leads to another. Since historical conditions changed after the early 1900s, was progressive thought a successful strategy in dealing with new conditions as well as old? This is to admit the logical meeting of past and present in historical study, for the reputation of progressive thought rests upon its success in the historian's present as well as in the historical past. Does progressive thought seem a wise or good intellectual strategy for dealing with past and present reality, as we now understand it? We are not belittling the real achievements of progressive reform thought if we locate certain problems in it, nor are we slighting the right of an earlier age to its own wisdom if we do not find its wisdom to be ours. In the sense of a present perspective on the past, one may speak of a scholarly analysis of the assumptions, methods, and value judgments of twentieth-century social thought as being both historical and contemporary, illuminating both the past and present.

This study will proceed through biographical sketches of various intellectuals—philosophers, journalists, scholars, and literary figures who illustrate the characteristics of the history under scrutiny.

CHANGE, PROGRESS, AND THE PROBLEM OF VALUES:
JAMES HARVEY ROBINSON

It may at first seem paradoxical that historians during the early 1900s, professionally preoccupied with the past, should have articulated one of the most popular rationales for present change. Yet such was the case. During the first half of the twentieth century, a group of scholars now called progressive historians were as important as any other intellectuals in explaining to their educated countrymen why old beliefs and habits should be replaced by new ones.

James Harvey Robinson (1863–1936) was one of the oldest and most famous of these reform-minded scholars who created the progressive interpretation of history. As a young historian he had followed the customary late nineteenth-century path of graduate training in Germany after earlier work at Harvard. As a professor specializing in medieval and early modern European history during the 1890s, Robinson expressed no particular interest in contemporary social reform or in the use of historical scholarship as an instrument for changing society. But after 1900 Robinson altered his perspective on both past and present, at roughly the same time as his younger colleague at Columbia University, Charles Beard, and Vernon Louis Parrington, Carl Becker, and Frederick Jackson Turner started to write progressive interpretations of American history which reigned supreme in the scholarly literature until around World War II. As their name suggests, progressive historians tended to equate historical change with progress. They saw conflict as the stuff of history, and there were temporary reverses as well as permanent gains, but on the whole the story of man was the story of progress. Phrased most generally and baldly, progressive scholars viewed science, experimentalism, rationalism, secularism, and democracy as the forces of light guiding mankind away from the historic forces of darkness: organized religion, supernaturalism, traditionalism, and aristocratic despotism. The progress by which progressive historians saw man advancing was increasing understanding of, adjustment to, and mastery over, his environment. Thus science stood as the crowning achievement of the human intellect, and the scientific or experimental method of inquiry was the device for the future reform of society.

The source of the popular appeal enjoyed by progressive historians rested in their heightened sense of contemporary relevance. "The present has hitherto been the willing victim of the past," wrote Robinson in The New History, in 1912, but "the time has now come when it should turn on the past and exploit it in the interests of advance." Robinson wanted studies of the past to be socially useful to the present, rather than merely of interest to those with historical curiosity. The precise role for historical scholarship to play was the investigation of the origins of current ideas and institutions. By understanding how the existing order developed, it could be seen why and how to change it. Historical investigation would show that the practices and policies of the present emerged in order to cope with environmental conditions in the past which for the most part no longer obtained. "Our respect for a given institution or social convention may be purely traditional and have little relation to its value, as judged by existing conditions," Robinson argued. "We are, therefore, in constant danger of viewing present problems with obsolete emotions and of attempting to settle them by obsolete reasoning."

It can be seen that in Robinson's plea for reform-oriented histories the social role of scholarship was primarily destructive, in the sense that it was to show by implication (if not explicitly) the irrelevance of certain contemporary inherited ideas and institutions to contemporary conditions. Man had progressed from past to present, but the continual problem of the present was the incongruity of inherited beliefs and habits on one side and new conditions on the other. Thus, individualistic creeds of self-help which satisfactorily coped with certain problems in agrarian life might be shown to deal unsuccessfully with urban problems. Yet if people were so tied to traditional ideas, no matter how irrelevant to the present, today's problems would go unsolved. Poverty, overcrowding, disease, and illiteracy in city ghettos would be tolerated as long as Americans refused to acknowledge that new city conditions demanded new beliefs concerning the proper role for government to play.

Despite the persuasiveness of the progressive argument, it is precisely at this point that the greatest ambiguity and most pressing problem occurred. Was the reformer's solution simply to make ideas and institutions mirror current conditions? Robinson often spoke as if this were the case. "Only a study of the vicissitudes of human opinion," he stated, can reveal the remoteness of the origins of our present beliefs and so "enable us to readjust our views so as to adapt them to our present environment."[2] But what concept of mind, what ideal function of values, did this imply? It did indeed imply that ideas and values ought merely to reflect external conditions. This was an unlikely position for a moralistic reformer, and Robinson in fact must be considered ultimately ambiguous on this question. For the ideas which he admired most in men's history were not simply mirrors of external conditions, but examples of innovative, new, "creative thought." The most impressive examples of "creative intelligence" to Robinson were modern scientific ideas, "the most striking instances of the effects of scrupulous, objective thinking." He was obviously not expecting to find human betterment only in making the mind the mirror of society, but also and contradictorily in the power of independent, rigorous, and imaginative thought to discover what was true and good. "It is this kind of thought that has raised man from his pristine, subsavage ignorance and squalor to the degree of knowledge and comfort which he now possesses," Robinson stated in *The Mind in the Making* in

2 James Harvey Robinson, *The New History* (New York: Macmillan, 1912), pp. 24, 22, 103.

1921. So strongly on this occasion did he accent the power of ideas to cause change, and so emphatically did he praise this power, that he wrote that "history, *namely change*, has been mainly due to a small number of 'seers,'—really gropers and monkeyers—whose native curiosity outran that of their fellows and led them to escape here and there from the sanctified blindness of their time."

The point of interest is not so much that Robinson was inconsistent, but the reasons for his inconsistency. Why did he sometimes say that social reform would best be served by bringing policies and practices into accord with environmental conditions, and at other times say that man had to master his environment through independent thought? Robinson was not aware of (or if aware, was not concerned about) the inconsistency because of his faith in progress. He believed that man's environment and his ability to deal with it were improving. He assumed that if man adjusted old beliefs to new conditions, it would constitute an improvement in beliefs. This crucial assumption lays bare the heart of progressivism. Enlightened thought and the external world were viewed as evolving together. It did not occur to Robinson to ask the value question: Are human environments always, or even usually, good? Is it normally acceptable to speak of getting in tune with one's surroundings, unless one has already passed a favorable moral judgment on them? The great optimism of Robinson's position is suggested by his attitude toward industrialism, urbanization, and increased communication. The industrial revolution provoked "unsuspected possibilities of social readjustment and the promotion of human happiness," he wrote:

> Associated with these same economic changes is the development of world-commerce and of incredibly efficient means of communication, which have brought mankind together throughout the whole earth in a spirit of competition, emulation, and co-operation. It will not be many years before every one on the face of the globe can read and write and be in a position through our means of intercommunication to follow the course of events in every portion of the earth. This astonishing condition of affairs suggests boundless possibilities of human brotherhood.[3]

Robinson was no consistent determinist, however, as we have seen, and he knew that men had to be rallied to take advantage of the opportunities offered by the favorable external environment. Hence he devoted himself to reform, convinced that

---

[3] James Harvey Robinson, *The Mind in the Making* (New York: Harper, 1921), pp. 55, 48–49, 79–80, 126.

the long-disputed sin against the Holy Ghost has been found; it may
be the refusal to cooperate with the vital principle of betterment.
History would seem, in short, to condemn the principle of conservatism as a hopeless and wicked anachronism.[4]

This quotation illustrates why it has been said that the progressive aca-
demics were reformers first and scholars second.

James Harvey Robinson made historical study seem excitingly relevant to the present by explaining how it could contribute to social reform.
Investigation of the origin and development of ideas and institutions in the
past would demonstrate their close relationship to past environmental
conditions and the practical ability of earlier policies and practices to meet
earlier needs. The reader of such a history would be able to see, if the
historian did not himself point out the implication, that the new conditions
of life under which the reader lived demanded new ideas and institutions.
An urban and industrial society in the twentieth century posed problems
which could not be dealt with by old formulas. But because Robinson saw
change from old to new as virtually synonymous with improvement, he
failed to pose the question which must in retrospect seem most profoundly
troubling. What is the role of value choice for man? Mere adjustment of
morals to facts is not good enough, unless the facts are themselves always
good. For later Americans who became increasingly worried about the
facts of life, increasingly dubious that progress was a fact of life, and
increasingly skeptical concerning human nature, Robinson's statement of
the human condition came to seem inadequate.

CHANGE, DISILLUSIONMENT, AND PROGRESS: WALTER LIPPMANN, I

Born a quarter-century after James Harvey Robinson, Walter Lippmann (1889—) was one of the youngest of the intellectual reformers who
achieved national prominence before the United States entered the war in
1917. A graduate of Harvard, where he had been president of the Socialist
Club, Lippmann by the ripe age of twenty-five was a member of the first
group of editors of New Republic, in 1914, and was recognized as one of
the country's most provocative social thinkers.

Lippmann, along with his fellow editors Herbert Croly and Walter
Weyl, had been critical of Woodrow Wilson's conception of the New
Freedom in the presidential election campaign of 1912 because it seemed
to Lippmann to represent a nostalgia for the American past, a past which
could not be recaptured. Wilson sensitively perceived the personal
anonymity and lack of equality of economic opportunity which had re-

---

[4] Robinson, The New History, p. 265.

sulted from increasing bigness, but Lippmann argued that Wilson's New Freedom, despite its well-intentioned reformism, furnished no solution except old Jeffersonian laissez-faire individualism. Like James Harvey Robinson, Lippmann insisted that new urban and industrial conditions demanded new public policies. For this reason, the men who were to become *New Republic* editors were most sympathetic to Theodore Roosevelt's New Nationalism.

Lippmann was convinced that the method of modern science, with its formulation and testing of hypotheses, was the instrument for moving society forward. Conservative defenders of the status quo, and even some reformers such as the Wilsonians who clung to Jeffersonian individualism, were trapped by outworn traditions. "We can no longer treat life as something that has trickled down to us," Lippmann wrote in *Drift and Mastery* (1914). "We have to deal with it deliberately, devise its social organization, alter its tools, formulate its method, educate and control it." He accented the need for mastery over the environment, and the ability of the experimental method to deal purposefully with man's problems. "Rightly understood," he said, "science is the culture under which people can live forward in the midst of complexity, and treat life not as something given but as something to be shaped."

On the eve of World War I, Lippmann's enthusiasm for the scientific method was coupled with a faith in democracy. "There is nothing accidental then in the fact that democracy in politics is the twin-brother of scientific thinking," he wrote. "For when the impulse which overthrows kings and priests and unquestioned creeds becomes self-conscious we call it science." The equation of democracy with science revealed the depths of Lippmann's optimism in prewar days, for he imputed the highest intellectual qualities to democratic man. And indeed Lippmann did have explicit praise for many Americans who, he said, had already abandoned nineteenth-century individualism in favor of a scientific democracy. Numerous leaders in business, labor, and government had shown awareness of the need for a scientific, planned, cooperative, and stable economic environment. With an optimism and rhetoric characteristic of prewar reformers, he declared the existence of a pervasive public interest. "The real news about business, it seems to me," Lippmann wrote, "is that it is being administered by men who are not profiteers." He emphasized that the new managers of big corporations were not the owners. "The motive of profit is not their personal motive."[5] Similarly, influential labor union leaders realized that not class warfare but cooperation through negotiation represented the course of mutual prosperity. And the fact that everyone was a

---

[5] Walter Lippmann, *Drift and Mastery* (Englewood Cliffs, N. J.: Prentice-Hall, Spectrum Books, 1961), pp. 147, 151, 43.

consumer constituted a further tie which united rather than divided the interests of a nation of individuals and groups. Upon such optimistic assessments of the early twentieth century, the progressive mind developed.

Prior to World War I, Lippmann assumed the promise of democracy insofar as he took for granted an intelligent public which had access to accurate information. He assumed the social success of the experimental method insofar as he took for granted that new knowledge and public policies would be an improvement over what they replaced. Lippmann's confidence was first undermined by World War I.

Reflecting on the national hysteria that followed Woodrow Wilson's call for a war to make the world safe for democracy, Lippmann questioned the rationality of the masses of men. Reflecting on the inaccuracy of information concerning the war that was available to the public, he questioned the democratic mass media.

The fanatical way in which Americans suppressed antiwar dissidents, legally through legislation and litigation and illegally in vigilante action, naturally caused many prewar reformers to revise their optimistic assessment of the behavior of Americans. This revision was no doubt accelerated in the 1920s by increasing numbers of intellectuals who concluded that the war had not really been worth fighting, that the United States had no genuine interest in it, and that Wilson's call for Americans to make the world safe for democracy was more appropriately designed for a medieval crusade than for twentieth-century foreign policy. In Lippmann's own view, American intervention was justified but on grounds of American self-interest and preservation of Europe's balance of power, not on grounds of Wilson's exaggerated idealism. Yet, whatever the rationale for war, Americans threw themselves into it with an irrational zeal which shocked many intellectuals, particularly in retrospect.

Dismaying in a different way to Lippmann was his conclusion after the war that the public was given little accurate information on which to base its judgments concerning the war and the peace conference. In *Liberty and the News* (1920) he argued, following a survey of newspaper coverage, that governments manipulated, in the name of national interest, the flow of information to the public, and that newspapers were at best careless and inaccurate in their news reporting and at worst cooperated with governmental censorship. It seemed to Lippmann that "the newspaper is in all literalness the bible of democracy," since democratic freedom of opinion was inconsequential unless the information upon which people built opinions was correct.[6] If the press failed in its responsibility, what chance then had democracy?

---

[6] Walter Lippmann, *Liberty and the News* (New York: Harcourt, 1920), p. 47.

What hope one might have salvaged from Lippmann's analysis of public misinformation, on the grounds that the press, and not the people, were responsible, was dispelled by his pioneering study of *Public Opinion* in 1922. It expressed a further disenchantment with democracy. "It is no longer possible, for example, to believe in the original dogma of democracy," he wrote, "that the knowledge needed for the management of human affairs comes up spontaneously from the human heart."[7] What was needed to deal with the complex modern world was not intuition nor sentiment nor tradition but analytical intelligence. But Lippmann argued that the thinking of most men was so crude, warped, and biased as to be almost inevitably and hopelessly ignorant, quite irrespective of the availability of accurate information. Lippmann's conclusion augured poorly for any appeal to democratic man. Consequently he suggested in 1925 in *The Phantom Public* that the public should not play a direct role in government. The measure of disillusionment after the war for Lippmann and other prewar progressives is made clear by a comparison with earlier reform programs which embodied direct democracy measures. Lippmann's common man in 1925 was to be appealed to only when public officials and political parties failed to agree on what to do.[8]

Doubts concerning the ability of the masses of men to govern themselves wisely were common currency among frustrated and disappointed reformers during the 1920s. What World War I had suggested, that the public was not necessarily rational and enlightened, the popular support for Harding and Coolidge in the postwar decade confirmed. It seemed to many old reformers that the people, after all, could not be trusted. Yet more profoundly disquieting, if further removed from practical affairs, was Lippmann's reduced enthusiasm in the 1920s for the immediate intellectual and moral results of the experimental method. Before World War I, at the height of Lippmann's optimism, he emphasized the role played by science in undermining traditional beliefs. But his assumption concerning change that the transition from old to new would constitute progress was then unqualified. By contrast, his explicit preoccupation as the postwar years advanced was not so much on what new and good would emerge but rather simply on the havoc wreaked by the collapse of traditional standards and morals. In 1929 he wrote *A Preface to Morals*, which surveyed the intellectual effects of the "acids of modernity." Instead of being stimulated by change and lack of stability, as he was before the war, Lippmann dwelled upon man's need for security. "Authority based on revelation once provided that foundation," Lippmann wrote, but the prestige "which

---

[7] Walter Lippmann, *Public Opinion* (New York: Macmillan, paper, 1960), pp. 248–249.

[8] Walter Lippmann, *The Phantom Public* (New York: Harcourt, 1925), p. 73.

once adhered to those who spoke by revelation, has passed to scientists." The problem was that science did not replace old moral truths with new ones. For "if civilization is to be coherent and confident it must be *known* in that civilization what its ideals are."[9] But the sources for all known ideals had been dissolved by the acids of science.

Nevertheless, despite Lippmann's disappointment over democracy and over the failure of modern scientific thought to yield new ideals, he continued throughout the 1920s to reveal an underlying faith in progress and a faith in the scientific method itself. Qualified though his hope was, he continued to argue that man had to persevere in the use of the same scientific inquiry which for the present was only adding to man's uncertainty and the chaos of knowledge. Lippmann made an absolute value of the experimental method of inquiry. "There is but one kind of unity possible in a world as diverse as ours," Lippmann wrote in 1920. "It is unity of method, rather than of aim; the unity of the disciplined experiment."[10] General disillusionment in the postwar years did not reduce his commitment to science. And general disillusionment did not erode his underlying faith that new ideals, new moral values, would some day emerge out of man's scientific knowledge. For example, speaking of the importance of understanding "the implications of the machine technology upon which our civilization is based," Lippmann prophesied in 1929 that when we acquired a proper understanding, "we shall discern the ideals of our industry in the necessities of industry itself." One can perceive an optimism as great as that of James Harvey Robinson when Lippmann adds that as "we discern the ideals of the machine technology we can consciously pursue them, knowing that we are not vainly trying to impose our casual prejudices, but that we are in harmony with the age we live in."[11] Emergent values were in the experimental method of inquiry, Lippmann continued to believe. As will be seen later, Lippmann was in fact at the end of the 1920s on the eve of a discovery of values to which he would be able to give full allegiance, just as he had hoped. But the nature of those values was to be quite different from what he had anticipated.

PRAGMATISM AND PROGRESSIVE VALUES: WILLIAM JAMES AND JOHN DEWEY

Historians of American social thought do not ordinarily invoke the names of philosophers. But progressive reform ideas are so often called pragmatic, and the early twentieth-century intellectual temper is so fre-

---

[9] Walter Lippmann, *A Preface to Morals* (Boston: Beacon, paper, 1960), pp. 133, 322.

[10] Lippmann, *Liberty and the News*, p. 67.

[11] Lippmann, *A Preface to Morals*, pp. 258–259.

quently characterized as philosophically pragmatic, that it is necessary to look at the official authors of theoretical pragmatism.

What was it about the philosophy of pragmatism that made it relevant to progressive social thought? Why was philosophic pragmatism so attractive to popularization, or even so susceptible to vulgarization, in the marketplace of social and political discussion? Superficially it might seem to be in part because, unlike most philosophers, William James (1842–1910) and John Dewey (1859–1952) intentionally addressed themselves in public lectures and essays to the educated layman on matters of general concern. But fundamentally it was because they successfully contributed a philosophic structure for the analysis of public issues and personal affairs as well as for metaphysical and scientific inquiry.

The first philosopher to make pragmatism fashionable among the intellectuals was William James, brother of the novelist Henry James. William James received a medical education at Harvard, then became a physiologist and a psychologist before finally turning to philosophy late in his career. His distinguished work in psychology formed perhaps the most important background for his philosophical pragmatism, for he approached pragmatism from his conception of how people formed their ideas. Indebted to Darwin, James felt that the Englishman's contribution was immense in suggesting that "almost all our functions, even the intellectual ones, [are] 'adaptations' and possibly transient adaptations, to practical human needs."[12] What this meant was that a discussion of human thought could not legitimately occur on an abstract level removed from practical conditions. "The use of the mind, which accounts biologically for its existence," James wrote in a Darwinian vein, "consists in its taking cognizance of the environment in behalf of the interests of the organism."[13] Ideas were born in an individual's attempt to overcome an obstacle, so that thought could properly be regarded as hypotheses designed to solve problems. Because James was convinced that the origin of thought was practical, he was likewise convinced that ideas should be discussed in terms of their practicality. Assuming that human thought originates in an attempt to take "cognizance of the environment in behalf of the interests of the organism," James opened the door to analyze ideas in terms of the effect they would have on the environment.

The most significant aspect of James's pragmatism for social thought, the pragmatic method, stemmed directly from his conception of the role of

---

[12] William James, *Collected Essays and Reviews*, R. B. Perry, ed. (New York: Longmans, 1920), p. 449.

[13] Quoted in Ralph Barton Perry, *The Thought and Character of William James*, vol. 2 (Boston: Little, Brown, 1935–1936), p. 76.

thought. The pragmatic method was a mode of inquiry, a means of discussion, which required that ideas or hypotheses or policies be analyzed in terms of their actual or projected consequences. Discussion of ideas in terms of their consequences was simply the reverse side of discussing ideas in terms of the practical conditions which caused them to be born. The pragmatic method was as applicable to a discussion of public housing possibilities or a legalized abortion debate as it was to an argument over God's existence or the nature of physical matter, although James did not himself apply the pragmatic method to social problems. He ordinarily emphasized the worth of the pragmatic method for scientific or religious or philosophical discussion, and in particular for separating the relevant from the irrelevant in the course of intellectual inquiry. If two ideas were in dispute, the pragmatic method "consists in auguring what practical consequences would be different if one side rather than the other were true," according to James. "If no difference can be thought of, the dispute is a quarrel over words."[14] Such an argument over ideas whose pragmatic consequences do not differ is, James said, "as unreal as if, theorizing in primitive times about the raising of dough by yeast, one party should have invoked a 'brownie,' while another insisted on an 'elf' as the true cause of the phenomenon."

Admitting that the pragmatic method revealed the futility of arguments as to whether elves or brownies raised dough, what about disputes in which the consequences of more than one proposition were true, yet different? Did the pragmatic method do nothing more than structure intellectual discussions in terms of consequences? It did nothing more, and James was clear on this point. The pragmatic method, James explained,

> has no dogmas, and no doctrines save its method. As the young Italian pragmatist Papini has well said, it lies in the midst of our theories, like a corridor in a hotel. Innumerable chambers open out of it. In one you may find a man writing an atheistic volume; in the next some one on his knees praying for faith and strength; in a third a chemist investigating a body's properties. In a fourth a system of idealistic metaphysics is being excogitated; in a fifth the impossibility of metaphysics is being shown. But they all own the corridor, and all must pass through it if they want a practicable way of getting into or out of their respective rooms.[15]

---

[14] William James, *Essays in Radical Empiricism*, R. B. Perry, ed. (New York: Longmans, 1912), p. 72.

[15] William James, "What Pragmatism Means," in *Pragmatism and American Culture*, Gail Kennedy, ed. (Boston: Heath, Amherst series, 1950), pp. 14, 15.

Everyone can go down the corridor discussing the practical consequences of various opinions. But the pragmatic method cannot decide for anyone which room he ought to enter, that is, which consequences are most desirable.

James hoped the pragmatic method would reform philosophical and religious discussion, as he argued it had already done in scientific inquiry. James's contemporaries in the early twentieth century, who were more preoccupied with public affairs and who were in addition sympathetic to social reform, quickly saw that the pragmatic method could be an instrument for reform. Proposals for change would of course be debated on the basis of their projected social consequences, but more important would be the pressure for change to which ideas and institutions of the status quo would be subjected. Existing policies and practices would have to be defended by their conservative supporters not on grounds of tradition or age alone, but also on the basis of coping with current conditions better than the alternatives posed by reformers.

Because the pragmatic mode of analysis was quickly used by reformers, as we have already seen in the case of James Harvey Robinson, the pragmatic method was the most significant contribution of the philosophy of pragmatism to progressive reform thought. It was no serious deficiency, as far as the reformers were concerned, that the pragmatic method lacked a value standard, a means by which good and bad could be discerned. For following use of the pragmatic method, the progressives applied their own reform goals. As Louis Hartz has said in his study of *The Liberal Tradition in America*, "It is only when you take your ethics for granted that all problems emerge as problems of technique."[16]

Among the philosophers, it was left to John Dewey, the other leading exponent of pragmatism, or instrumentalism as he preferred to call it, to ally explicitly that philosophy with social reform. James died in 1910 before the pre-World War I reform movement had reached its height, and in any case had never supported progressive reform. John Dewey lived until after World War II and remained an active reformer throughout his long life. As a young professor at Chicago he pioneered in educational reforms at the University's laboratory school; later at Columbia he was always deeply involved in current affairs. James' pragmatic method was designed to clear away the intellectual underbrush of outworn traditions in philosophy, religion, and science, and Dewey extended his focus to include aged social traditions.

Dewey's central theme for half a century was the need for applying the scientific, or experimental, or pragmatic, or instrumental method to

---

[16] Louis Hartz, *The Liberal Tradition in America* (New York: Harcourt, 1955), p. 10.

the world's problems. World War I, which swept him up at the time in support of American intervention and later resulted in his disillusionment, only sharpened Dewey's plea for an experimental approach to society. During the 1920s and much of the 1930s he consistently argued that contemporary man was living by old principles which were no longer relevant to present conditions. "Traditional ideas are more than irrelevant," Dewey wrote in 1929, "they are the chief obstacle to the formation of a new individuality integrated within itself and with a liberated function in the society wherein it exists." He did not stop to spell out the beliefs to be embodied in the new individuality, for he did not know what they would be except that they would be new, different, and good, and he was most concerned with undermining the old beliefs. "There is danger in the reiteration of eternal verities and ultimate spiritualities."[17] Today's world was a new environment that demanded application of the scientific or pragmatic method to test new hypotheses or policies. Dewey's plea was to find policies which would work in solving current problems. "The fundamental trouble, however," he wrote in 1931, "is not lack of sufficient information about social facts, but unwillingness to adopt the scientific attitude in what we do know."[18]

No more than James, when he formulated the pragmatic method, was Dewey preoccupied with working out criteria for determining the success of experimentation. He assumed it would be obvious what was good and what was bad. "A moral law, like a law in physics, is not something to swear by and stick to at all hazards; it is a formula of the way to respond when specified conditions present themselves," Dewey argued in *The Quest for Certainty* in 1929. "Its soundness and pertinence are tested by what happens when it is acted upon." Here once again is the faith of the progressive experimenter. The words used by Dewey as a test—"soundness" and "pertinence"—imply values. The test must be a test of something. Dewey of course knew this; he accepted the view of the progressive reformer that judgment would be easy. He did not spell out in detail the nature of new social values because during the 1920s and earlier 1930s he was uncertain about what might emerge. He emphasized pragmatic means more than social ends because, as optimistically as Walter Lippmann at the end of the 1920s, he hoped that experimental methods might uncover goals which were new in their details:

Operational thinking needs to be applied to the judgment of values just as it has now finally been applied in conceptions of physical

---

[17] John Dewey, *Individualism Old and New* (New York: Minton, 1929; Putnam, Capricorn Books, 1962), pp. 93, 147–148.

[18] John Dewey, *Philosophy and Civilization* (New York: Macmillan, 1931), p. 329.

objects. Experimental empiricism in the field of ideas of good and bad is demanded to meet the conditions of the present situation. . . . Men would think of themselves as agents not as ends; ends would be found in experienced enjoyment of the fruits of a transforming activity.[19]

It is not necessary to ask what kind of end or value is the "experienced enjoyment of the fruits of a transforming activity" in order to see that Dewey was caught up in enthusiasm for his method. His means were his ends insofar as he hoped that the experimental method would surely uncover new and good ends. Dewey was here most relativistic, but also most utopian.

Dewey's almost unlimited admiration for experimentation can be seen in his writings on the Soviet Union following a visit in 1928. Not an apologist for dictatorship when he perceived it, he sympathized with the Russians insofar as he could find experimentation occurring. He imputed to most Russians the same enthusiasm that he expressed when he spoke of the liberating effect of the scientific method. "The people go about as if some mighty and oppressive load had been removed, as if they were newly awakened to the consciousness of released energies," Dewey wrote. He did not find fixed Communist doctrines to be as significant as "the fact of this achieved revolution of heart and mind, this liberation of a people to consciousness of themselves as a determining power in the shaping of their ultimate fate." In praising the new spirit of change, he specifically minimized the importance of what current conditions and practices were, on the grounds that everything was in transition. Thus on one level it was implicitly suggested that a judgment of current conditions would be inappropriate, even as on another level an affirmative judgment was being made. The alleged experimentation was the key to both.

At the same time, Dewey's utopian hopes shone through occasionally as he described what he saw in the Soviet Union. "Perhaps the most significant thing in Russia, after all, is not the effort at economic transformation," he wrote, "but the will to use an economic change as the means of developing a popular cultivation, especially an esthetic one, such as the world has never known." It was as an educational revolution, in a broad sense, that Dewey was excited by in the Soviet Union, and his hopes were high. "I have never seen anywhere in the world such a large proportion of intelligent, happy, and intelligently occupied children," he said. Dewey admitted that in the great process of educating the Russian people to new ways of thinking, the Soviets had made education identical with

---

[19] John Dewey, *The Quest for Certainty* (New York: Minton, 1929), pp. 278, 258, 276.

propaganda. But he cautioned his readers to remember that for the Soviets "the end for which propaganda is employed is not a private or even a class gain, but is the universal good of universal humanity." Speaking specifically of the school system, and contrasting it with those in Western countries, Dewey was frankly envious. "The Russian educational situation is enough to convert one to the idea that only in a society based upon the cooperative principle can the ideals of educational reformers be adequately carried into operation."[20] These quotations suggest that Dewey was not only expressing support for experimentation, but also for specific values which he imputed to the Soviets. He noted in passing the fact of Communist political dictatorship, but he did not allow his negative judgment of it to undermine his celebration of the intellectual revolution which he attributed to the Soviets.

Because he had faith in the future, in man's ability to build a new and better world, Dewey dwelled upon the intellectual technique which would bring about change. Like Walter Lippmann, he hoped that the experimental method would yield new values. Like James Harvey Robinson, he tended to assume that change would equal betterment. For Dewey, as for most other reformers in the early twentieth century, pragmatic experimentation was accompanied by progressive assumptions concerning man and history.

SYMPATHETIC PRAGMATIC AND PROGRESSIVE INTERPRETATIONS OF
EUROPEAN DICTATORSHIPS IN THE 1920s:
WILLIAM HENRY CHAMBERLIN, I, AND LINCOLN STEFFENS

The previous discussions of Walter Lippmann and John Dewey have already suggested that the character of social thought changed in some respects as it moved into the 1920s. Lippmann's faith in democracy was undermined, and his confidence in science was qualified by its failure to yield immediately new values to replace the ones it eroded. John Dewey's favorable assessment of certain Soviet practices reflected his criticism of aspects of American society in the postwar years. In a slight way, Lippmann and Dewey mirrored larger patterns of thought among the intellectuals in the 1920s.

Prior to World War I, the assumptions and methods of progressive and pragmatic thought were accompanied by pervasive reform attempts within the fabric of the American democratic constitutional system. It was widely taken for granted that the established system was capable of making necessary and proper changes. The most vocal exception to this gener-

---

[20] John Dewey, *Impressions of Soviet Russia* .(New York: New Republic, 1929), pp. 4–5, 8, 31, 28, 54, 86.

alization was a small group of intellectuals who did not express confidence in the possibility of meaningful reform. A few of these were political radicals who thought progressive reform was too conservatively middle-class; more were writers and other artists whose interest in public policy was largely swallowed up by their personal and cultural concerns. The strains of both political and cultural radicalism, which before World War I were frequently expressed by the same people, manifested what historians call "the estrangement of the intellectuals." This phenomenon has been a recurrent feature of the last two centuries of European history, but it has been a more recent occurrence in the American experience. In the United States during the prewar years the alienated young intellectuals criticized American materialism, Victorian prudery which inhibited sexual relations, philistine artistic taste, the inhumanity and the dull sterility of life generally. The political system was indicted for perpetuating the economic and political status quo. Little magazines were formed as a vehicle for the intellectuals' art and opinion, and bohemian communities were organized in the cities to implement their counterculture. Generally optimistic concerning man's nature, hopeful about improving the human condition through experimentation, and assuming the progress of history, the estranged intellectuals held ideas that were in these respects within the prewar progressive and pragmatic climate of opinion. But in their more specific attacks upon the dominant life-style of the society, and in their political radicalism, the young bohemian intellectuals expressed their alienation.

A thin current of political radicalism among the estranged intellectuals survived into the 1920s, as shall be illustrated shortly, but the more common postwar manifestation of the alienation of the intellectuals was personal and cultural. The fabled "lost generation" of artists who expatriated themselves to Paris after World War I was in search of personal and artistic freedom. Writing from France in 1922, Harold Stearns told of the joys of not living in the United States:

> I read of tobacco being barred from Utah—but I read it with a cigarette in my mouth. I read of "rum" ships being seized and confiscated just outside New York harbour—as I sip my *Bordeaux blanc* on the terrace of a favourite cafe. I read of the "shimmy dance" being made a crime in some of our States—as I reflect upon whether or not I shall go to "Marcelle's" ball to-night, where all the ladies will be nude, and no one will be in the least disturbed. I read of "The Demi-Vierge" being ostracized from the New York stage— yet a few minutes later I am searching the quay, in the open sunlight, for my favourite book on flagellation.[21]

---

[21] "Letters from Abroad," *The Freeman* 5 (July 5, 1922):398.

Similarly, bohemian Malcolm Cowley recalled in *Exile's Return* the Greenwich Village creed in the postwar years:

1. The idea of salvation by the child. . . .
2. The idea of self-expression. . . .
3. The idea of paganism.—The body is a temple in which there is nothing unclean, a shrine to be adorned for the ritual of love.
4. The idea of living for the moment. . . .
5. The idea of liberty.—Every law, convention or rule of art that prevents self-expression or the full enjoyment of the moment should be shattered and abolished. Puritanism is the great enemy. . . .
6. The idea of female equality. . . .
7. The idea of psychological adjustment. . . .
8. The idea of changing place. "They do things better in Europe."[22]

Historians have emphasized the disillusionment and despair concerning America which was implicit, when not explicit, in the writings of the alienated literary intellectuals of the 1920s. It is only a qualification of that emphasis upon postwar disillusionment and despair to point out that the Harold Stearnses and Malcolm Cowleys retained a good deal of faith in their ability to make utopias out of their bohemias.

Both the postwar disillusionment and the utopianism can be seen in the career of William Henry Chamberlin (1897–1969), one of the intellectuals whose political views were radical in the 1920s. Chamberlin's youthful background prior to World War I was similar to most of the estranged young intellectuals who dreamed of Europe and scorned the philistinism of their own country. "I instinctively shrank," Chamberlin later wrote of his youth, "from the America of mechanical progress, commercial shrewdness, boisterous boosting which I saw around me." Reminiscing in his early forties, Chamberlin characterized his adolescence as "an unconscious process of spiritual emigration. My body was in America; my mind, for much the greater part of the time, was in some European land." "I cannot recall any American author, much less any American composer," he later wrote, "who exercised on me the fascination with which I was inspired by a score of European historians, novelists, philosophers, and musicians."

Chamberlin's newspaperman father voted Socialist in the years prior to World War I, and Chamberlin himself as a youngster was inspired by Theodore Roosevelt in the 1912 campaign. Initially an enthusiastic partisan of the Allies when the war broke out, Chamberlin became increasingly critical of both sides, and after the Russian revolutions of 1917 he cheered the Bolshevik withdrawal from the war. When Allied and Ameri-

---

[22] Malcolm Cowley, *Exile's Return* (New York: Viking, paper, 1951), pp. 60–61.

can troops intervened in Russia, he interpreted this as an unjustified attack upon the Bolsheviks, who had nobly renounced both war and capitalism. "I think 90 percent of my Bolshevik sympathy grew out of my bitterly hostile attitude toward the war," Chamberlin later asserted. Due to his home background, he had taken socialism for granted, and he made no special study of the ideas of Marx and Lenin until the 1920s. He reflected that "what made me a staunch partisan of the Soviet regime throughout the whole period of the Russian civil war was the feeling that here was the culmination of a triumphant revolt against a plot of the ruling classes in general and the capitalists in particular against the masses of soldiers of all nationalities who had been killed, wounded, gassed, maimed."[23]

From 1919 to 1922 Chamberlin, after marrying a Russian-born American girl who shared his sympathy for the new Soviet government, worked as a newspaperman in New York and devoted his spare time to reading news from Russia and writing pseudonymous articles in defense of the Bolsheviks. In 1922 Chamberlin and his wife decided to see for themselves what the Soviets were doing, and they went to Moscow for an intended visit of four months which turned out to be a stay of almost twelve years. Appointed Moscow correspondent for the *Christian Science Monitor*, Chamberlin remained until 1934, and he became, along with Louis Fischer and Walter Duranty, one of the chief American sources of information concerning the Soviet Union.

The significance of Chamberlin's interpretation of events in Moscow was that it offered a revolutionary alternative to the America of the 1920s. At a time in the United States when reform was dormant, European revolutionary governments became the focus of attention for Americans contemplating the wisdom of radicalism. From those such as Chamberlin who were sympathetic to the Soviet dictatorship there emerged a radical defense of revolutionary change.

When the Chamberlins arrived in Russia, Lenin's New Economic Policy was already underway, and Chamberlin's period of greatest sympathy for the Soviet Union lasted roughly as long as the NEP, which was abandoned in 1929. The New Economic Policy, which was regressive from a strictly theoretical Communist viewpoint, made concessions to capitalistic individualism in an attempt to improve economic conditions in a Russia devastated by war and revolution. Chamberlin's sympathies at the time were extended to theoretical communism and what he emphasized was the tension existing between Communist goals and NEP means.

Chamberlin's view of the Soviet Union during the 1920s can be characterized as a pragmatic and progressive defense of Communist expe-

---

[23] William Henry Chamberlin, *The Confessions of an Individualist* (New York: Macmillan, 1940), pp. 8, 12, 13, 42.

rimentation. It was explicitly pragmatic insofar as he frequently justified Soviet actions on the grounds that they worked, or should be given the chance to see if they would work. Crucial to this pragmatic defense was a relativistic assumption that one could not judge a foreign country such as Russia, or a revolution such as the Bolshevik, with the same standards one would apply to the United States. "A Western liberal is likely to be alienated at every turn by the dogmatic philosophy and the rough methods of the Russian Communist," Chamberlin admitted in 1923, but the necessities of the situation made "rather academic" the "question whether there was a moral justification for the dictatorship."[24] The masses of people had not known freedom of any kind in the past, and the Communists were effecting an economic revolution which brought "social liberties" which were "probably more valuable" than such political liberties as the right to vote for rival parties or to have a free press. "Liberty," he added, "is always a relative and personal conception."[25]

But Chamberlin's explicit pragmatic relativism was nothing more than a confident gloss covering an absolute faith in progress and a commitment to the success of communism. During the 1920s he was not a detached observer neutrally reporting the strange habits of a foreign species. Chamberlin was convinced the Soviets were successfully implementing good changes. To a significant extent, even though limited by their lack of political power, Russian workers had a democracy. "Only the most progressive American unions have gained a degree of control over working-conditions comparable to that possessed by the Russian factory-committees," Chamberlin reported in 1923, and the Russians had the important advantage that off the job they were not subject to the influence of their capitalistic employers.[26] As he wrote, following a tour of a socialized factory which had been confiscated from a Franco-Belgian firm:

> Walking through the factory one felt the new spirit of fraternity that the Revolution has brought to Russia. The old servility and cringing before the boss had all disappeared with the going of the Tsar and the coming of the Soviet power. The workers were free men, and knew it.[27]

---

[24] "A Working-Class Aristocracy," *The Freeman* 6 (Feb. 14, 1923):537.

[25] "Liberty in the Soviet State," *Atlantic Monthly* 144 (October 1929):551, 552. See also "Russia's Balance Sheet of Democracy," *The Freeman* 7 (March 28, 1923):56–58.

[26] "The Emerging Factory in Russia," *The Freeman* 6 (Feb. 7, 1923):513, 515.

[27] A. C. Freeman (Chamberlin's sometime pseudonym when writing articles which he thought might offend his regular employers, the *New York Tribune* before he went to Russia and the *Christian Science Monitor* afterwards), "A Revolutionary Factory," *The Freeman* 8 (October 10, 1923):107.

Near the end of the 1920s, Chamberlin realized that the factory democracy he earlier cherished had not been copied throughout the society, and
the Party bureaucracy had largely replaced the Tsarist aristocracy.
"Classes still exist in Russia," he admitted, "but their make-up is more
fluid than in any other country." Most important was the sweeping revision in values which was brought by the Bolsheviks, and which earned
Chamberlin's admiration:

> If the really decisive test of the significance and permanence of a
> revolution is to be found in the changes it brings in social institutions
> and in moral and intellectual conceptions, the Russian Communists
> may reasonably claim authorship of one of the great revolutions, if
> not of the greatest revolution, in history.[28]

The significance of Chamberlin's belief in progress was that it allowed him to reconcile Soviet difficulties and deficiencies with his generally favorable assessment: today's blemishes would be removed tomor-
row. He recognized that economic production in most areas during the
1920s was less, or only slightly better, than it had been before the Revolution. But improvement was made each year in most areas, and the line of
progress seemed infinite.

Similarly, Chamberlin admitted the problem of Party dictatorship,
but he optimistically foresaw its disappearance. "The present dictatorship,
which unquestionably has its harsh and ugly sides," he wrote in 1923,
"will in all probability be softened when the Communists no longer feel
themselves in the position of sailors compelled to employ drastic measures
in order to save a sinking ship."[29] As soon as the Soviet Union was
completely secure from enemies within and without, there would be no
need for the dictatorship. As an indication of his faith in Communist
theory as well as his belief in progress, Chamberlin postulated further that
the more completely socialistic the economy became, the less political
factionalism would occur. "With a few more years of evolution it may
well come about that the Russian people will rub their eyes some morn-
ing," he wrote in 1923, "and find out that instead of experiencing the
ruthless dictatorship of a political party, they are living in a state that has
shed its political coat altogether and that is functioning chiefly as an
organ of economic administration."[30] Thus did William Henry Chamberlin reject American society, pragmatically defend Soviet experimentation,
and at the same time reveal his progressive faith in the possibility of

---

[28] "The Balance Sheet of Bolshevism," *The American Review of Reviews* 78 (October
1928):405, 408.
[29] "Russia in Reconstruction," *The Freeman* 7 (Nov. 7, 1923):203.
[30] "The Future of Soviet Russia," *The Freeman* 8 (Dec. 19, 1923):348.

reconstructing society. He had constructed an intellectual rationale in defense of revolutionary change, in support of dictatorial means which were cleansed by the purity of the ends. Without this rationale, Chamberlin would have been forced to judge the means themselves, and the judgment would have to have been unfavorable.

The Soviet Union attracted the most admiration during the 1920s, but it was not the only European dictatorship to be viewed sympathetically by American intellectuals. Mussolini's Italy, too, received some favorable attention in the postwar decade. The same pragmatic and progressive rationale was articulated by Lincoln Steffens (1866–1936) in defense of the Fascists as in defense of the Bolsheviks.

Steffens first gained fame as a muckraker in the early years of the century. He was one of a group of journalists, including Ida Tarbell, David Graham Phillips, Gustavus Myers, and Upton Sinclair, who stimulated popular interest and sympathy for reform through their articles and books exposing greed and corruption in business and politics. Steffens during the prewar progressive era shared much of the characteristic optimism expressed by James Harvey Robinson, Walter Lippmann, and other intellectuals, concerning the probability that America could reform itself within the traditional democratic constitutional system. But, as Christopher Lasch has shown in The New Radicalism in America, Steffens was no more than Robinson or Lippmann simply a moralistic do-gooder. Even in the early days of reform enthusiasm, "Steffens came to the conclusion," according to Lasch, "that what was needed, if American society was to be made over, was not a moral awakening but a better appreciation of American society—not morality but 'intelligence.' "[31] Further, if one accepts Lasch's interpretation of Steffens, even as a muckraker Steffens was profoundly alienated from middle-class society and thus was in quest of radical alternatives.

Following World War I, Steffens decided that revolutionary Europe rather than reformist America offered a more intelligent hope for change. He lived in Europe during the 1920s, observed and interviewed revolutionary dictators, and offered a progressive and pragmatic justification for their existence. Like William James or John Dewey when contrasting primitive religious creeds and modern science, Steffens counterposed moralistic democratic liberalism and the facts of modern political life. In his Autobiography published in 1931, Steffens portrayed his education gained by watching the dictators as a movement from conventional American ignorance to empirical knowledge. Mussolini and the Bolsheviks had not been bound by old values and moralistic shibboleths which would

---

[31] Christopher Lasch, The New Radicalism in America (New York: Knopf, 1965), p. 266.

have prevented them from effecting change. They practiced dictatorship because they looked at the facts of human behavior and saw what worked:

> Mussolini was challenging axioms, which brain-bound me, which spiked Europe to the past. As bold as Einstein, Mussolini, the willful man of action, saw by looking—at Russia, for example—that the people there in power were distracted by conflicting counsel and helpless. They wanted to follow, not to lead; to be governed, not to govern themselves. Democracy enthroned went straight to a dictatorship. He saw also about the same time, in a similar emergency— in the fright of war which is like that of a revolution—the western nations turned to dictatorship. England made Lloyd George a dictator; France made Clemenceau a dictator; the United States suppressed its Constitution and made Woodrow Wilson absolute. But I, too, saw that. We all saw it, as Mussolini did. What was the difference? I—we—judged what we saw. We said Wilson weakened, Lenin did wrong. Mussolini saw it all; he said it, but also he acted upon it. He really learned it all.[32]

Progressive reformers in the United States had been restricted by their absolute, unexperimental belief in democratic constitutionalism from seeing how to change society.

Steffens acknowledged that the dictatorial means used to effect new goals were different from the goals themselves, but he was sympathetic in the 1920s to change, and he deprecated any invocation of moral judgment which interfered with change. Liberty, for example, he thought was a "psychological matter," something which all peoples abolish when it conflicts with any value they really desire. "Isn't liberty a measure of our sense of security and nothing else?" Steffens asked. "Like democracy, like honesty, like peace, liberty has to be founded in economic arrangements that abolish fear."[33] Like William Henry Chamberlin, Steffens was enunciating a relativistic conception of value; depending upon the circumstances, men cherished various goods and excoriated different evils. Steffens was not worried about dictatorial deprivation of human freedom, because he was sympathetic to the social change which he hoped would occur. The boundlessness of his hope is revealed by the fact that although he described the Bolshevik plan for a classless society, Steffens never suggested what he thought Mussolini was attempting to bring about. Change for the sake of change was enough; means took precedence over ends.

---

[32] *The Autobiography of Lincoln Steffens* (New York: Harcourt, 1931), p. 816.
[33] *The Autobiography of Lincoln Steffens*, p. 818.

Despite the obvious disillusionment with American democracy which is implied by Steffens' and Chamberlin's defense of revolutionary dictatorship in Europe, their thought in the 1920s was marked as much by progressive faith as by despair. Like John Dewey and Walter Lippmann, Chamberlin and Steffens assumed that new and good values would emerge from the experimental method. As James Harvey Robinson assumed that to understand the facts of industrialization would be to discover new values in those facts, so Steffens assumed that to understand what people did would be to know what they ought to do. Since neither Steffens nor Chamberlin was an amoral man, their lack of concern with a standard of value judgment can be explained only by their confidence that the movement of history was in a progressive direction. Experimentation would consequently yield progressive values. It was a final measure of their progressive faith and their optimism that the European dictatorships were interpreted by Chamberlin and Steffens as experiments, applications of the scientific method to social problems.

3
THE DISCOVERY OF EUROPEAN TOTALITARIANISM IN THE 1930s

The prewar progressive and pragmatic thought of men such as Walter Lippmann, James Harvey Robinson, and John Dewey did not die out in the postwar decade, and, as Clarke Chambers has argued in *Seedtime of Reform*, "neither were the years of the twenties the wasteland for reform that they have frequently seemed." Campaigns for child labor legislation, government aid for dependent children, women's rights, improvement of slum conditions, municipal reform, and progressive education were among the many reforms supported by various groups of Americans after the war. Yet it remains true that the "climate of the 1920s was just not hospitable to the extension of reform measures," as Chambers adds, "or to the initiation of new programs."[1] It was not until the stock market crash of 1929 precipitated the Great Depression of the 1930s that a new public mood provided the opportunity for wide-scale reform.

Franklin Roosevelt campaigned in 1932 on a platform which was not much different from Herbert Hoover's, except for the Democratic plea for the end of prohibition and for

---

[1] Clarke Chambers, *Seedtime of Reform* (Minneapolis: University of Minnesota Press, 1963), pp. 26, 89.

lower tariffs; Roosevelt criticized the President during the campaign for excessive federal spending. During the first three months in office FDR came up with a mixed program which cut veterans' pensions and government employees' salaries, on one side, and, on the other, attempted to stimulate the economy through public works and aid to the unemployed. Big business was helped by allowing restriction of production to keep prices up, on the one hand, while organized labor was given the theoretical right to bargain collectively with employers, on the other. Roosevelt, in short, at the outset had no specific plan. Yet by 1935 the drift leftward of the New Deal was clear. A national social security program, a firm guarantee of collective bargaining for labor, a more steeply graduated federal income tax, and various federal aid programs for the economically disadvantaged meant that Roosevelt had inaugurated the welfare state by the end of his first term. Welfare-state planks which had appeared only in the Socialist party's platform in 1932 had been enacted into law within a few hectic congressional sessions. Roosevelt's second term ensured the permanence of the achievements of the first term, and neither later Democrats nor Republicans would dismantle the New Deal.

The attitude of most intellectuals toward the New Deal during the early and middle 1930s ranged from sympathetic support to radical criticism from a perspective to Roosevelt's left. Only during the second term, and especially as the election of 1940 neared, did FDR gain overwhelming support from the nation's intellectuals, and this was due in large part to the enemies Roosevelt had made by this time among businessmen and other conservative opponents of the New Deal. Earlier it was common among intellectuals to criticize FDR for his lack of systematic planning along socialistic lines. "Experimental method is not just messing around nor doing a little of this and a little of that in the hope that things will improve," John Dewey wrote in 1935 in obvious criticism of Roosevelt. Dewey pleaded that "ideas and theory be taken as methods of action tested and continually revised by the consequences they produce in actual social conditions."[2] It was a characteristic pragmatic argument, and Dewey, who voted for Norman Thomas in 1932 and 1936, had in mind testing specifically socialistic hypotheses. However fondly the American intellectual community would look back upon the New Deal after World War II, Roosevelt's policies seemed to many at the time to fall far short of desirable social changes.

Radicalism of one sort or another received considerable support among intellectuals in the 1930s. The Soviet Union was the magnet for much of the radical thought, and the Communist party of the United States was the beneficiary of the attraction. From an approximate 8000

---

[2] John Dewey, "The Future of Liberalism," *The Journal of Philosophy* 32 (April 25, 1935):228.

dues-paying members in 1930 the Party reached a possible 100,000 members in 1939. Not a large number even at its height, the Party exercised an influence among intellectuals which was out of proportion to its membership. For some who were sympathetic to the Party, the Communists seemed to be merely more radical New Dealers. Whereas from the late 1920s to 1935 it was the official policy of international communism to oppose socialist, liberal, and other parties around the world, from 1935 to 1939 this policy was reversed. As a part of an anti-Fascist crusade, Communists in all countries during this period joined in a Popular Front with reform parties such as the New Deal. "Communism is Twentieth-Century Americanism" became a Popular Front slogan. For some who were sympathetic to the Party, worldwide revolution looked attractive and the Soviet Union served as the model revolutionary state. The American intelligentsia generally viewed revolution more sympathetically, particularly in the early 1930s, than it had for almost a century.

The radical thought of some of the intellectuals, and the reform achievements of the New Dealers, have been properly emphasized in the histories and recollections of the Depression. Nevertheless, from a later perspective, the long-range intellectual significance of American social thought in the 1930s does not lie in the decade's preoccupation with radicalism and reform. It rests rather in the essentially conservative foundations which the 1930s laid for the 1940s and 1950s. This can be seen through an examination of the impact of the "discovery" of totalitarianism on the part of the intellectuals who had earlier been sympathetic to revolutionary dictatorships, and the intellectuals' consequent celebration of traditional America.

THE DICTATORIAL DREAM THAT FAILED: WILLIAM HENRY CHAMBERLIN, II

Chamberlin's estrangement from America, his criticism of the Allied effort during World War I, his sympathy for the Bolshevik revolution, and his progressive and pragmatic defense of the Soviet dictatorship in the 1920s have been reviewed in the previous chapter. But in the early thirties Chamberlin became one of the first American intellectuals to turn against Stalin.

What seems to have caused Chamberlin's public disillusionment with the Soviet Union was Stalin's replacement of Lenin's New Economic Policy with the Five Year Plan, beginning in 1929. The Five Year Plan represented a "hard" line leftward toward complete collectivization, which had its greatest impact during the early 1930s. Under the NEP, the Russian peasantry had not been forced into collective farms, but the Five Year Plan enforced socialization. The lands of well-to-do peasants, or kulaks, were confiscated, and millions of kulaks were removed to slave labor camps or liquidated. The mass of the peasantry was forced onto collective farms under Communist management. Peasant recalcitrance, poor management, and heavy government requisitioning of the resulting low agricultural yield led to widespread famine during 1932–1933.

Chamberlin's criticism of the Five Year Plan was not immediate, probably because the full effects of thorough collectivization were not at once apparent. When Chamberlin first reported the deportation and elimination of the kulaks in 1931, he reported the brutality of the policy but he did not dwell on it, and he added that there was as yet no new food shortage and that agricultural socialization seemed to be successful.[3] When the famine of 1932–1933 did occur, however, Chamberlin concluded that inhumane means were accompanied by disastrous results: widespread starvation and a pervasive worsening of living conditions. Henceforth the logic of Chamberlin's earlier support for the Soviets spun in reverse. His former pragmatic tolerance of Communist dictatorship was dependent upon the assumption of progressive goals. It was taken for granted that socialization was economically superior. But when Chamberlin decided that collectivization hampered economic growth instead of fostering it, he no longer justified inhumane means. The ends were now determined to be bad. As Chamberlin recoiled from the suffering he saw, for the first time he located the source of Soviet problems in the dictatorial repression of human rights. The famine of 1932–1933 could not have happened if there had been a free press and free election, Chamberlin said in 1934, because Russians who possessed full information about the starvation would then have demanded changes in the government's economic policy.

After 1933 Chamberlin developed at length a critique of the Soviet Union "as an example of historical tragedy of the deepest and truest type, a tragedy of cruelty, of the crushing out of innumerable individual lives, not from sheer wanton selfishness, but from perverted, fanatical idealism —always the surest source of absolute ruthlessness." He saw the fatal weakness of bolshevism in its "conviction that the end justifies the means." Failure to feed the Russian people was the apparent provocation for Chamberlin's withdrawal of support from the Communists, but his indictment was phrased in terms of absolute morality. And as soon as he had changed his standard of judgment from a relative to an absolute one, he lumped the Soviet dictatorship with the Fascist dictatorship:

One among many points of faith common to apologists of Communism and of Fascism is an overweening contempt for civil liberties,

---

[3] "Balance Sheet of the Five Year Plan," *New Republic* 66 (February 25, 1931):41–44.

which are represented as unnecessary and inconvenient barnacles on the ship of progress. The longer I have lived in the Soviet Union, where civil liberties—freedom of speech, press, assembly, and election—are most conspicuously lacking, the more I have become convinced that they are of vital and tremendous importance, and that their existence or absence is as good a test as any of the quality of a nation's civilization. The Communist (or the Fascist—their trend of thought in this question is strikingly similar) talks of civil liberties as of the outworn fetish of a handful of disgruntled intellectuals who are unable to rise to the necessary vision of the high and noble character and purpose of the Communist (or Fascist) state.[4]

Chamberlin had not forgotten how idealistic and inspiring were the professed goals of the Communists, and he emphasized in 1935 that these, and the differing sources of support in the population, comprised the main contrast between the Soviet Union and Nazi Germany. But differences in theory were undermined, he now said, by similarities in "political technique, administrative practice, and ruling-class psychology." Both Communist and Nazi parties were dictatorial, and their leaders had absolute power, he argued, and the religious fanaticism in both parties, particularly of the younger generations, was similar. Both states, according to Chamberlin in 1935, were "totalitarian."[5]

He had always followed, and occasionally reported, events in Germany, but it was only after his disillusionment with the Soviet Union and Hitler's accession to power that Chamberlin began to focus upon Germany jointly with Russia as the major threat to freedom. He objected in 1935 to "the double standard of morals" applied by Westerners sympathetic to the Soviet Union:

> Isn't there something fundamentally unsound, even ridiculous, in the mental processes that lead many non-communists to apply to Russia an ever condoning, ever mitigating, soft and mild standard of judgment, while applying to the systems of Mussolini and Hitler and also to democratic regimes a merciless severity of moral judgment that suggests Jonathan Edwards, hell fire and eternal damnation?[6]

From the perspective of human liberty, it made no difference whether despots of the Left or of the Right violated basic civil liberties, according

---

[4] "Farewell to Russia," *Atlantic Monthly* 154 (November 1934):564–573, 566–567.

[5] "Russia and Germany—Parallels and Contrasts," *Atlantic Monthly* 156 (September 1935):349, 367.

[6] W. H. Chamberlin, letter to editor, *New Republic* 82 (February 27, 1935):77.

to Chamberlin by the mid-1930s. Writing in 1936, he said that his long residence in Russia and his brief visits to Germany had forced him "to the conclusion that the most important issue which confronts civilization in the present century is that of democracy versus dictatorship." He specifically added that this issue "transcends in importance the lesser economic question of the relation between public and private enterprise."[7] Chamberlin's rejection of the "collectivist" or "totalitarian" state, and his embracement of "liberal democracies" with their protection of civil liberties, was unambiguous.[8] Chamberlin, by the middle of the Depression decade, had expressed his full disillusionment with the Soviet dream, renounced revolutionary dictatorship of the Left as well as that of the Right, called Stalin's, Hitler's, and Mussolini's rule "totalitarian," and was on his way to a new celebration of American traditions.

Advocacy of an isolationist foreign policy was the expression of Chamberlin's embracement of the United States during the last half of the 1930s. It came to seem to him by the late thirties that impending war in Europe would doom civilization on that side of the Atlantic but that the future civilization could be America's if "only America will have the common sense and self-restraint not to yield to foreign-inspired propaganda, and not to waste the lives and substance of its people in fighting foreign quarrels. . . ." Chamberlin argued in his autobiography, *The Confessions of an Individualist* (1940), that war was justifiable only to repel direct attacks against national security, and that therefore the United States had no reason to intervene either in Europe or in Asia. Modern war, he stated, always dehumanized life and robbed the individual of his liberty, regardless of the noble aims for which wars were purportedly fought. Chamberlin increasingly insisted upon the priority of individual freedom against the encroachment of the State, and by the end of the decade called himself "an enthusiast for every guaranty of personal liberty contained in the Bill of Rights and the American Constitution." Economic individualism, too, came by 1940 to be linked in Chamberlin's mind with his desired social order:

> . . . I should unhesitatingly say that political democracy, associated with a predominantly individualist economic order, has proved the most promising means of insuring the best material conditions for

---

[7] Introduction, dated November 1936, to *Collectivism: A False Utopia* (New York: Macmillan, 1937), p. v.

[8] Chamberlin's choice of the word "collectivist" at this time was meant to indicate a political concept common to communism and fascism, in which "the state owns the people." Chamberlin did not mean an economic concept. He used the word "totalitarian" infrequently at this time, but his definition of it seems synonymous with "collectivism." See *Collectivism: A False Utopia*, pp. 171, 186.

the greatest number of people, the highest cultural standards, and the least objectionable functioning of the state.[9]

This did not mean that Chamberlin was uniformly opposed to Roosevelt's New Deal, prior to World War II, but it did mean, as he put it in 1940, that he was "skeptical of those moves which look toward a planned economy."

It had been a long intellectual journey for William Henry Chamberlin since the 1920s. Traveling widely throughout the world, and almost never living in the United States, he moved from a position of pro-Communist radicalism to one of support for the existent American political system, which included the New Deal. Confident as a young man, following World War I, that Bolshevik change could be equated with progress, he became increasingly pessimistic concerning the possibility of social progress in the world by the end of the 1930s. "I am afraid the omens almost all point to the twentieth century as an age of retrogression," Chamberlin wrote in 1940, "of decline to constantly lower levels, culturally and materially, through a more and more disorderly and senseless series of wars and revolutions."[10] Sure in the 1920s that Communist revolutionary dictatorship was roughly equivalent to scientific social experimentation, Chamberlin during the later thirties increasingly argued that the virtues of human society stemmed from the absolute value of the individual. Abandoning the dream of human reformation, and fearing that the world might get worse rather than better, William Henry Chamberlin, on the eve of World War II, praised American institutions for contributing to liberty and hoped that the United States could isolate itself from the international conflagration.

MARXISM AS PRAGMATISM AND THEOLOGY: SIDNEY HOOK, I

To the extent that the interpretations of the Soviet Union expressed during the 1920s and 1930s by Lincoln Steffens, William Henry Chamberlin, and John Dewey were sympathetic, they were all variations on a common progressive and pragmatic theme. The essential view was the same, regardless of whether the observer (such as a Chamberlin) was a long-time resident and close student of Russia, who knew the language, or whether he (as Steffens) was quickly passing through the Soviet Union, or (as in most cases) had never been to Moscow at all. The facts, and the

---

[9] W. H. Chamberlin, *The Confessions of an Individualist* (New York: Macmillan, 1940), pp. 261, 303.
[10] Chamberlin, *Confessions*, pp. 259–260, 297.

process of acquiring facts, were less important than the preconceived categories into which the facts were placed.

The radical in America who discussed Marx and communism most philosophically in the 1930s was Sidney Hook (1902—). His interpretation was as progressive and pragmatic in outlook as that of others sympathetic to the Soviet Union. Born and raised in New York City, and a professor of philosophy at New York University for more than forty years, Hook was a student and interpreter of the philosophy of John Dewey. During the early 1930s, when he was most sympathetic to Marxian communism (he supported the Communist party candidate for the presidency in 1932), Hook tried to render Marx American, pragmatic, and specifically Deweyan. "I believe it is possible," Hook wrote in 1934, "to present dialectical materialism as a plausible scientific philosophy which might be described in the technical idiom of contemporary Anglo-American philosophy as experimental, evolutionary naturalism."[11]

Hook's most important pragmatic interpretation of dialectical materialism was his insistence that Marxism was a philosophy of action in which human beings and their ideas played a creative role. Hook objected to deterministic interpretations of Marx which accentuated the causal power of economic conditions to the exclusion of human volition except as a reflex to material forces. Marx's conception of cognition, argued Hook, was that man's perceptions were not merely inner carbon copies of an outside reality. Further, Marx held a multiple causation interpretation of history in which man's ideas were one part, the economic factor another part, and these parts (as well as others) pragmatically and dialectically interacted. Thus he avoided materialistic determinism even as Marxism stipulated that economic factors were "in the last instance," or "in the last analysis," decisive. "What justifies Marx and Engels in holding that the mode of economic production is the *decisive factor* in social life," wrote Hook in *Towards the Understanding of Karl Marx* (1933), "is the revolutionary will of the proletariat which is prepared to act upon that assumption." In other words, Hook said that the idea of a successful revolution in the minds of the proletariat was crucial; thus he was able to argue that Marx emphasized the role of thought. At the same time, the belief in successful revolution was based wholly upon a belief in the hypothesis that economic conditions are the decisive causal factor in social change.

To a critic Hook's statement might appear to be a blend of circular

---

[11] "Communism Without Dogmas—A Reply," in Bertrand Russell, John Dewey, Morris Cohen, Sidney Hook, Sherwood Eddy, *The Meaning of Marx: A Symposium* (New York: Farrar, 1934), p. 126.

reasoning and positive thinking. Translated into nonpragmatic terms it could be said to mean that capitalistic economic conditions will be the decisive causal factor in a revolution *if* the workers revolt in an attempt to abolish capitalistic economic conditions. To Hook, however, what might seem to others to be no more than an affirmation of hope was a legitimate pragmatic synthesis in the tradition of Dewey. What Hook was saying was that the truth of a proposition is to be judged by the practical consequences of acting upon the assumption that it is true. He spelled out the argument in *Towards the Understanding of Karl Marx*:

> It is only because we want to change the economic structure of society that we look for evidence of the fact that in the *past*, economic change has had a profound effect upon all social and cultural life. Because we want to change the economic structure of society, we assert that this evidence from the *past* together with our revolutionary act in the *present* constitutes a sufficient cause for believing that the general proposition "in the last instance the mode of economic production determines the general character of social life," will be true in the near *future*.[12]

Hook's description of Marxism shows that he combined, in characteristic pragmatic fashion, statements referring to the past (in which human actions were complete) and statements referring to the future (in which human actions were still to be determined), when he stated historical generalizations or laws. Historical generalizations or laws were to this extent similar to scientific laws. In addition to *describing* Marxism in pragmatic terms which blended past and future, Hook also erected a similar pragmatic test for *evaluating* the accuracy or truthfulness of Marxism: ". . . the test of the truth of historical judgments about the past is to be sought in the concrete historical activities of the present, and their future results." More specifically, "the validity of Marx's method depends upon whether it enables us to realize the class purposes in whose behalf it was formulated."[13] All of this constituted a remarkable mixture of philosophical pragmatism and revolution, attempting to meet the demands of both—however theoretically.

Sidney Hook, like Chamberlin and Steffens and any other humane person expressing sympathy for revolutionary violence, had to face the problem of bad means used in the name of good ends. Hook defended in

---

[12] Sidney Hook, *Towards an Understanding of Karl Marx* (New York: John Day, 1933), pp. 181–182. Italics in the original.

[13] Hook, *Towards an Understanding of Karl Marx*, p. 6.

theory the revolutionary Communist who used violence to suppress class enemies, on the basis that the goal of true democracy could not be achieved while class enemies existed. "During the transitional period the denial of liberties is directed, in theory at any rate, only against those whose activities are such as would restore the old order and therewith destroy the new freedom and liberties which the social revolution has won," Hook wrote in 1934.[14] "Revolutionary terrorism is the answer of the proletariat to the political terrorism of counter-revolution," he stated in *Towards the Understanding of Karl Marx*. "Its ruthlessness depends upon the strength of the resistance it meets. *Its acts are not excesses but defensive measures.* Its historical justification is the still greater tragedies to which it puts an end."[15] Hook qualified his endorsement of revolutionary violence but his qualifications revealed his commitment to the proletariat rather than to the inextricability of means and ends. He stipulated that violence and suppression were justified only against class enemies, and only on behalf of the majority, that is, the proletariat. If these conditions were met, according to Hook in 1934, "the use of force does not constitute a special moral problem but a problem in effective and intelligent application." Notably absent from Hook's discussion at this time was concern for, or even any reference to, rights of individuals who dissented from the majority. Traditional law was dismissed as self-interested guarantees for the class enemy. "If the use of force is justified only when it has the sanction of legality," Hook argued, "then it can be pointed out that those who have the legal power can always change the forms and meaning of 'legality.' The consequence would be a necessary acceptance of any regime so long as it abided by its own shifting forms of legality."

Since Sidney Hook was consistently concerned with making Marxism philosophically pragmatic, and since philosophical pragmatists were characteristically conscious of the corrupting influence which bad means have on good ends, an explanation is needed for why this awareness was so often absent from his thought in the early 1930s. The explanation lies in Hook's faith in revolutionary communism at the time. His discussion implied a dichotomy between utopian communism, which he defended exclusively in terms of its ideals and whose violent means he explicitly justified because of its noble ends, on the one hand, and, on the other, traditional Western governmental systems, which he criticized in terms of the discrepancy between their reality and their ideals. His hardheaded analysis, which exposed the inevitability of an undemocratic reality behind the ideals of "capitalistic" societies, was in contrast even to his critique of the

---

[14] "Communism Without Dogmas—A Reply," p. 113.
[15] Hook, *Towards an Understanding of Karl Marx*, p. 305. Italics in the original.

bureaucratic dictatorship of the Soviet Union. Hook was not a defender of Party bureaucracy, which he blamed for betrayal of the Russian revolution, but as late as the middle of the thirties he allowed the ideals of revolutionary communism to distinguish the Soviet dictatorship from that of the Fascists. "The dictatorship of the Fascist Party is an essential part of the political system of fascism and is the only way by which capitalism can preserve itself against disintegration," Hook wrote, whereas, "the dictatorship of the Communist Party bureaucrats is a foreign excrescence upon the structure of the workers' state as well as upon the true communist party."[16] In other words, it was not as significant that the practical consequences in the two cases yielded a similar dictatorship as it was that the *goals* were dissimilar. To be sure, Hook was not saying that the ends justified the means in this particular instance, as he steadfastly refused to justify the dictatorship of the Party *over* the proletariat. But, in evaluating Soviet Russia, he distinguished means from ends, declaring the ends favorable by themselves. On this basis, he was able to contrast the Soviets with the Fascists, whose means and ends he insisted were inseparable.

Hook's faith in revolutionary communism cannot be separated from his harsh view of capitalism, Western parliamentary government, and the United States. Belief in the desirability of the former was functionally related to hostility to the latter. Hook denied that Western representative, constitutional systems of government constituted anything more than a subterfuge created by capitalism. Because "the socio-economic process" is the "chief independent causal factor" behind politics, said Hook in 1934, "the fundamental issue of modern times is not democracy versus dictatorship but capitalism versus communism."[17] The first set of alternatives was illusory because under capitalism only the bourgeoisie benefited. "From the point of view of the worker, the political democracy of the bourgeoisie meant the social *dictatorship* of the bourgeoisie," he wrote.[18] In this respect, it makes no difference to the worker "when the Fascists today call for political dictatorship or their liberal opponents call for the retention of political democracy."[19] Thus the second and true set of alternatives only, between capitalism and communism, offered the possibility of choosing democracy for everyone.

The ideals of the Declaration of Independence, according to Hook, could only be implemented in a classless society. Speaking at the University of Virginia on July 4, 1934, he assailed contemporary American society:

---

[16] "Communism Without Dogmas—A Reply," pp. 110, 141.
[17] "On Workers' Democracy," *Modern Monthly* 8 (October 1934):529.
[18] "Communism Without Dogmas—A Reply," p. 76.
[19] "On Workers' Democracy," p. 530.

If we still believe in equal opportunity for all and in the equal right of all citizens to life, liberty, and the pursuit of happiness, how can we give any measure of support to a social order which despite an overabundance of the conditions for a good life, dooms millions upon millions to physical degradation, psychological insecurity, and moral despair; which drives other millions to death and injury in foreign and civil war for the sake of profit; and which makes the development of individuality and personality depend upon the possession of material wealth?[20]

It has been seen that Hook's utopian faith in revolutionary communism during the early 1930s was the driving force behind his pragmatic interpretation of Marxism and his relativistic defense of violent suppression of class enemies by the proletariat. Hook often made a distinction, however, between his ideal of revolutionary communism and Soviet practice. As the 1930s advanced, the discrepancy between the two gradually eroded Hook's faith in the ideal and transformed his attitude toward the United States. In 1934, even as he wrote that "only communism can save the world from its social evils," Hook vehemently attacked the official Communist party in Russia for despotic suppression of dissident proletarian opinion. If one remembers that he was in theory still willing to sanction the silencing of class enemies, one can imagine the anger behind Hook's disillusioned statement that the official Party throughout the world no longer deserved to be called "Marxist, critical or revolutionary."[21] During the middle 1930s, he often attacked "apologists of Stalinism," pro-Stalin critics of Trotsky, and defenders of the Purge trials.[22]

By the later 1930s, Hook no longer allowed the superior theoretical claims of communism to distinguish the Soviet Union from Nazi Germany and Fascist Italy. As he increasingly lumped all the dictatorships together, his respect for the United States as a guardian of democratic constitutional government perceptibly increased. The word "democracy" was as pervasive in Hook's writings at the end of the decade as earlier, but the word no longer meant the same thing. Formerly democracy meant economic equality, as in occupation or salary, but by 1938 it was defined politically: "A democratic society is one where the government rests upon the freely-

---

[20] Printed as "The Democratic and Dictatorial Aspects of Communism," in *International Conciliation* (December 1934):463.

[21] "Communism Without Dogmas—A Reply," p. 144.

[22] See "Manners and Morals of Apache-Radicalism: Some Comments on Mr. Herberg and Other Apologists of Stalinism," *Modern Monthly* 9 (June 1935):199–204; "Liberalism and the Case of Leon Trotsky," *The Southern Review* 3 (Autumn 1937): 267–282; "Corliss Lamont: Friend of the G.P.U.," *Modern Monthly* 10 (March 1938):5–8.

given consent of the governed."[23] Two years later, Hook elaborated his political definition in *Reason, Social Myths and Democracy*:

> There is common agreement that democracy as a way of life can flourish only when differences of opinion can be negotiated by free, critical discussion in which those who at any time, and on any question, are a minority, may become the majority, provided they abide by democratic processes.[24]

Hook explicitly confronted and rejected his old economic approach to democracy through complete state planning when he commented in 1940 that those countries with the most democratic political and social life had the least centralized economic systems. "There is both irony and pathos in a situation," Hook wrote, "in which socialists of many countries look back with nostalgia to the freedoms of the capitalistic democracies they had once considered their mortal enemy."[25]

Hook's enthusiasm for the scientific method, and for a pragmatic social philosophy, also remained undiminished at the end of the decade but the enthusiasm came to be expressed differently. It would not be an exaggeration to say that for Hook the experimental method became the intellectual equivalent of the democratic constitutional process. As he came to defend democratic politics as a system of critical discussion of public issues, so he interpreted the scientific method to embody absolute freedom and to depend for its existence upon a free society. The very process of scientific inquiry, like that of democratic constitutionalism, was celebrated by Hook. This amounted to an assertion that the morality of means were inextricably bound to the morality of ends. In 1940 he complained in *Reason, Social Myths and Democracy* that "there is no room in a totalitarian culture for the scientific approach, with its critical probing of alternatives, when questions arise concerning the social ends and values which guide major national policies."[26] Bad means would inevitably corrupt good ends. He criticized those, such as Max Lerner, who continued to contrast favorably the Soviet Union with Nazi Germany and who thus were surprised and shocked by the nonaggression pact of August 1939. Hook attacked Lerner for being willing "to use or condone any method of

---

[23] See "Democracy as a Way of Life," *The Southern Review* 4 (Summer 1938):47.

[24] Sidney Hook, *Reason, Social Myths and Democracy* (New York: John Day, 1940, 1950), p. 9.

[25] "What Is Living and Dead in Marxism," *The Southern Review* 6 (Autumn 1940):315.

[26] Hook, *Reason, Social Myths and Democracy*, p. 10.

achieving and holding power for avowedly good causes like 'socialism' without reflecting upon the consequences of those methods on the character and direction of power so achieved."[27] Hook also began to criticize the theories, as well as the practices, of Communists. No longer did he consider dialectical materialism to be a science, but instead a "theology."[28] He began to deprecate the extent to which Marxists (rather than Marx) supported economic determinism. The gap between theory and Soviet practice began to close for Hook, and he became increasingly critical of both. He pointed out in *Reason, Social Myths and Democracy* that Lenin thought transition to socialism could not be achieved either democratically or peacefully, leading Hook to conclude that "Lenin's responsibility for Stalin is absolute."[29] Trotsky was declared to be potentially guilty of Stalin's kind of despotism.[30]

Hook's embracement of America as a democracy in a world challenged by totalitarianism was complete enough by the end of the 1930s for him to articulate what was essentially a wartime ideology, and which he would not significantly change later. By the decade's end Hook had developed the foundation of his Cold War position on free speech, by which authorities were justified in suppressing speech of those alleged totalitarians who would allegedly deny it to others if in power. "Effective defense against a foreign totalitarian enemy may require extraordinary and exceptional measures of co-ordination and control," he wrote in 1940. He admitted that such state control might itself be "the road to totalitarianism," but declared that "the alternative is *certain* totalitarianism."[31]

Hook, like Chamberlin, had rejected the radicals' rationale with its pragmatic defense of what they hoped would be progressive revolutionary change. Further, both men had developed an idea of totalitarianism as the embodiment of absolute social evil: the subjugation of the human personality by the State. They concluded that good ends could not justify bad means, that the traditional value of the dignity of the individual forbade support for totalitarianism. Locating the evil of totalitarianism in the European dictatorships, Chamberlin and Hook by the late 1930s em-

[27] Review of Max Lerner, *Ideas Are Weapons, Partisan Review* 7 (March–April 1940):159.

[28] "Reflections on the Russian Revolution," *The Southern Review* 4 (Winter 1939):441.

[29] "What Is Living and Dead in Marxism," in *Reason, Social Myths and Democracy,* p. 302.

[30] "Reflections on the Russian Revolution," in *Reason, Social Myths and Democracy,* p. 461.

[31] "The Democratic Way of Life," in *Reason, Social Myths and Democracy,* p. 288.

braced America in a way which forecast the outlines of social thought during the 1940s and 1950s.

OLD AND OUTWORN VALUES BECOME NEW AND RELEVANT:
WALTER LIPPMANN, II

The cases of William Henry Chamberlin and Sidney Hook are representative of the more extreme reversals in ideological position which took place among intellectuals on the Left during the Depression. If less dramatic than the perception of totalitarianism by those who were formerly faithful followers of a revolutionary dictatorship, the development of a concept of totalitarianism was a significant event for any intellectual. As Walter Lippmann's career attests, one's intellectual universe could be transformed by the idea of totalitarianism regardless of one's former attitude toward the revolutionary dictatorships. Lippmann's shift from confidence to disillusionment has been reviewed in the previous chapter. Before World War I he believed that the rational, experimental method would overcome society's problems; after the war, though disillusioned, he thought that this same scientific approach could somehow uncover new human values.

Lippmann discovered the values he had been searching for in the 1930s, and they turned out to be some of the old traditional ones which he had earlier characterized as anachronisms or had simply taken for granted. As the dictatorships of the world increased during the 1930s both in number and ruthlessness, Lippmann fell back on the traditional values of a liberal society. In 1933 his previously characteristic concern with social planning from the top gave way to new criticisms of collectivization and a defense of American liberalism. As late as March 1933, in a talk at Berkeley which was published the same year as A New Social Order, Lippmann primarily emphasized the need for Americans to create an "ordered society" with "a great common purpose, disciplined to act together, educated to understand and respect superior knowledge, ready and eager to follow and to honor the leadership of our best men."[32] Though lacking specifics, this sounded like a call to support the New Deal at the very least, if nothing more centralized than that. And in the early months of the New Deal, Roosevelt had Lippmann's support. But the latter soon saw the much-discussed economic planning of the New Deal against the background of Hitler, Stalin, and Mussolini. By May of 1934, when Lippmann delivered the Godkin lectures at Harvard, upon which he had been working since the summer of 1933, he strongly condemned "utopian" collectivist planning and advocated "a policy which is frankly and un-

---

[32] Walter Lippmann, A New Social Order (New York: John Day, 1933), pp. 20, 21.

ashamedly middle class in its ideal." Published as *The Method of Freedom* in 1934, the Godkin lectures suggested Lippmann's new ideological position.

In his argument, he tried to get down to fundamentals. In spite of the particular economic conditions of the Depression, he stressed that current crises must not be allowed to tempt Americans to forget basic ideals of civilized life which would remain valid when transitory problems were forgotten. Lippmann obviously intended to suggest how "the method of freedom" had to be integrally related to the goal of freedom. "For policies and programs are only instruments for dealing with particular circumstances," he wrote. "Purposes and ends embodying a conception of the good life and of what makes for dignity in human existence are older than all our working principles and will survive them." Lippmann granted that the State had to intervene to a greater extent than previously, in order to "overcome the disorders of capitalism," and he admitted that a conflict existed in the United States between human rights and giant corporation rights. "But the issue between the giant corporation and the public," Lippmann added, "should not be allowed to obscure the truth that the only dependable foundation of personal liberty is the personal economic security of private property." He scoffed at the idea of a classless proletarian society, both because it was fantastic to imagine transforming selfish individuals into "individuals who are devoted only to the abstract general good," and because propertyless citizens would be powerless in the face of an omnipotent state. A middle-class society, in which "most people" own private property, offered the best hope for the protection of human freedom. Lippmann was critical of those New Deal creations, like the National Recovery Administration and the Agricultural Adjustment Administration, which gave legal protection to monopoly rather than to competition, and he was unwilling to accept the view that the majority of Americans necessarily knew best what was good for them. But he was not in *The Method of Freedom* explicitly ópposed to the New Deal. He expressly favored governmental intervention in the economy whenever necessary to "compensate" for imbalances in the private sector. Further, he specifically added "the right of access to remunerative work" to the list of rights which he thought all civilized states ought to protect, along with "rights of personal liberty, rights of political participation, rights of property, rights of local self-government."[33]

What Lippmann was inveighing against was the thoroughgoing collectivism of the European dictators. He made this clear in *The New Imperative*, written after he delivered the Godkin lectures, and published

[33] Walter Lippmann, *A Method of Freedom* (New York: Macmillan, 1934), pp. 91, 99, viii, 101, 91, 99, 107.

the following year. Protesting against "the spell cast by the European revolutions," Lippmann insisted that America had to forge a policy which escaped the "alien stereotypes" of fascism and communism, and which at the same time heeded "the new imperative" to maintain the people's standard of living. "I have convinced myself at least that we are on a road which is not the Berlin-Moscow road," he wrote in 1935, "that we are evolving a method of social control which is not that of *laissez-faire* and is not that of a planned and directed economy." His praise of the New Deal was to this extent clear, if only implicit. But he criticized "advanced New Dealers" who were "half-seduced" by the model of the Bolsheviks, as well as "conservatives" who mistakenly thought that "all public control leads to communism."[34] To develop his argument that Americans could cope with the Depression while avoiding the sins of European revolutionary extremism, Lippmann tried to show that Hoover, rather than Roosevelt, had actually initiated the welfare-state principles which the New Deal had broadened. This argument concerning the fundamental "conservatism" of Roosevelt's policies, which later became and still remains the orthodox historical interpretation of the New Deal (without stressing as Lippmann did the similarities of Hoover to FDR), was in praise rather than in deprecation. Yet Lippmann remained wary of New Dealers who did not share his awareness of exactly what they were doing, or to put it differently, of the extent to which they had created a grab bag of measures rather than a systematic policy. Lippmann's wariness was exemplified by his public support for Alf Landon rather than Roosevelt in 1936.

By 1937 Lippmann had completed his major book on the nature of the humane civilization which embodied the values destroyed by what he called the "collectivist movement" or the "totalitarian regimes." Begun in 1933, approximately at the time he began working on the Godkin lectures, *The Good Society* was a development of the argument initiated by *The Method of Freedom*. And in view of his vote for Landon in 1936, when Lippmann was still writing *The Good Society*, it is impossible not to read the book also in part as an indictment of tendencies which he thought were present in the New Deal—despite his lack of more than passing concern with the Roosevelt administration. It is impossible too not to read the book as a reversal of much of the direction of Lippmann's earlier writings during the second and third decades of the century. Instead of the youthful, *au courant*, sophisticated approval of intellectual currents, particularly those fashionable in Europe, which marked his books between 1913 and 1929, *The Good Society* responded with a loud and old-fashioned "no" to what was going on in the world, particularly in Europe.

---

[34] Walter Lippmann, *The New Imperative* (New York: Macmillan, 1935), pp. 4, 5, 6–7.

What made Lippmann's denunciation appear so sweeping as to include the New Deal was his criticism of all those "men who call themselves communists, socialists, fascists, progressives, and even liberals," who "are unanimous in holding that government with its instruments of coercion must, by commanding the people how they shall live, direct the course of civilization and fix the shape of things to come." It was this pervasive mood of increased governmental authority as the only conceivable path of public policy which Lippmann decried. The major source of his concern was not Roosevelt's New Deal, however much it shared unfortunate collectivist tendencies, but the despotisms of Stalin, Hitler, and Mussolini. Dictatorships of Left and Right were fused by Lippmann into an idea of totalitarianism:

> Though despotism is no novelty in human affairs, it is probably true that at no time in twenty-five hundred years has any western government claimed for itself a jurisdiction over men's lives comparable with that which is officially attempted in the totalitarian states. No doubt there have been despotisms which were more cruel than those of Russia, Italy, and Germany. There has been none which was more inclusive. In these ancient centres of civilization, several hundred millions of persons live under what is theoretically the absolute dominion of the dogma that public officials are their masters and that only under official orders may they live, work, and seek their salvation.[35]

In a chapter on "the totalitarian regimes" he dismissed the argument that "the concentration camp, the secret police, and the censorship" of the dictatorships were merely transitional. As a practical matter, according to Lippmann, the government was never secure enough to dispense with repression. "The emergency never ends: the transition cannot be completed until everyone is a fascist or a communist by instinct and indurated habit." The totalitarian state was thus a permanent evil, and even a threat to those outside it; the regimentation of society was inevitably related to militarism. The logic culminating in war inhered in the nature of economic collectivization, said Lippmann, because only under conditions of permanent crisis could total economic planning be maintained. He did not make clear why a government could not sustain the necessary support for collectivism without actually going to war. But much more importantly, Lippmann was attacking a sacred cow of those who were at all sympathetic to the Soviet Union, when he denied that Russia was essentially pacifistic in

---

[35] Walter Lippmann, *The Good Society* (New York: n.d.; page references are to Grosset & Dunlap's Universal Library paperback), pp. 3–5.

the 1930s. It was commonly assumed in Left and liberal circles that whatever Stalin's sins, aggressiveness in foreign relations was not one of them; fascism, on the other hand, was customarily viewed as expansionist by nature. Lippmann stressed the basic similarities common to totalitarianism of Left and Right. He argued that belligerence in external affairs was essential to communism as well as fascism. In this as in so many other respects he anticipated during the 1930s what was to become the dominant American view of the late 1940s and 1950s.

The guidelines for positive action set down in *The Good Society* were much closer to those of the New Deal than Lippmann's general strictures against "gradual collectivism" would suggest. He recognized the abuses of the status quo prior to the New Deal and insisted that they be remedied: inequality in wealth out of proportion to any justifiable standard of merit; monopolistic and variously corrupt violations of equality of economic opportunity; inferior public education; excessive private exploitation of natural resources; insufficient public regulation of private business; and inadequate public works and public recreation facilities. To pay increased costs of governmental progress Lippmann advocated more steeply graduated income taxes and high inheritance taxes. But, and this was at the heart of his reformed liberalism, he argued that an attempt should be made to ascertain and to tax most heavily "unearned" income gained through "the various kinds of monopoly, from exclusive rights in land and natural resources, from bad markets in which the ignorant and the helpless are at a disadvantage." For these unearned incomes "are not the wages of labor or management, the interest on capital, or the profits of enterprise, as determined in free and efficient markets, but tolls levied upon wages, interest, and profits by the subversion or the manipulation of the market price for goods and services." As Lippmann recoiled from the growing threat of totalitarianism throughout the world, he sought refuge in a humane liberalism.

The history of freedom in the modern world, according to Lippmann, had been the history of liberalism, that is, of the individual's emancipation from centralized authority. He did not consider it legitimate to reject the theory of economic and political liberalism merely because during the late nineteenth and the twentieth centuries liberalism had wrongly been used to justify the existing order. "In its vigorous periods liberalism has always meant rebellion against oppression and a determination to police aggression and acquisitiveness," he wrote. "Liberalism, therefore, is not the doctrine of laissez-faire, let her rip, and the devil take the hindmost." Above all, liberalism rightly understood has meant an absolute dedication to constitutionalism and the protection of civil liberties. For the "liberal state is to be conceived as the protector of equal rights by dispensing justice among individuals," said Lippmann. "It seeks to protect men against arbitrariness, not arbitrarily to direct them." Its roots could be traced to the conviction that the individual was inviolable:

> . . . it is here that the struggle between barbarism and civilization, between despotism and liberty, has always been fought. Here it must still be fought. The self-evident truth which makes men invincible is that inalienably they are inviolable persons.[36]

The good society was therefore a liberal society, governed by a constitutionalism which protected individual rights, which offered economic self-improvement through equal opportunity, and which was based upon the absolute sanctity of human life.

Like William Henry Chamberlin, Lippmann by the late 1930s had defined the evil of totalitarianism as it was embodied equally in fascism and communism, and the virtue of liberalism particularly as it was found in American traditions. Both Chamberlin and Lippmann, like Sidney Hook, described the world conflict at the end of the decade in terms of democracy versus dictatorship. But though Chamberlin and Lippmann wrote at length concerning the proper role of the United States in world affairs after the late 1930s, they saw in the ideas of totalitarianism and liberalism dramatically different implications for American foreign policy. Lippmann expressed his defense of liberal democracy by urging that American security be protected through a commitment to Great Britain. He expressed his opposition to totalitarianism by calculating pragmatically how any totalitarian regime at any particular time threatened the security of the United States. While Chamberlin advocated a policy of American "isolation" in World War II, Lippmann was an "interventionist" on behalf of the Allies prior to Pearl Harbor.

The approach of World War II confirmed for Lippmann the correctness of his previous interpretation of World War I. American interests seemed indissolubly connected to Great Britain; in particular to friendly Britain's ability to control the other side of the Atlantic. Lippmann commented in 1937 on the ironic nature of the recent neutrality legislation, which was intended to be "isolationist." He noted that its "cash-and-carry" provisions meant that in case of war the United States would again be trading only with the British (because England's enemies would not possess the sea power to come to American shores). Lippmann suggested that it seemed impossible to escape the Anglo-American alliance. "In the

---

[36] Lippmann, *The Good Society*, pp. 55, 225–226, 355, 367, 375.

final test, no matter what we wish now or now believe," he wrote in 1937, "though collaboration with Britain and her allies is difficult and often irritating, we shall protect that connection because in no other way can we fulfill our destiny."[37] Lippmann continued to develop the same argument, with greatest urgency, as the Germans conquered the continent. In *Life* magazine, on July 22, 1940, he insisted that "The Economic Consequences of a German Victory" over Great Britain would be disastrous to the interests of the United States. "The plain fact of the matter is that if Britain falls, then Europe, Asia and Africa will be ruled from Berlin, Moscow and Tokyo," Lippmann wrote. "The American manufacturers will then be allowed to supply the totalitarian hemisphere with those products in which the totalitarian empires are temporarily deficient—as a matter of fact, to supply them with those products which will be immediately necessary in order to make totalitarian industry entirely independent of American industry."[38] By the spring of 1941, as Lend-Lease supplies were being shipped to Britain, he considered American intervention a fact, and he praised it. As in World War I, he said, America intervened at that point when it appeared Great Britain could not by herself control the European shore of the Atlantic. Most Americans know "that for their physical security, for the continuation of the free way of life, it is necessary that the other shore of the Atlantic Ocean should be held by friendly and trustworthy powers."[39] As these quotations show, Lippmann's view was that armed opposition to German "totalitarianism" was required when the possibility of British defeat threatened American security. Russia remained "totalitarian" but even in the period of the Nazi-Soviet pact, from August of 1939 to June of 1941, Russia did not in Lippmann's mind constitute an immediate threat to the security of the United States. Thus, Lippmann presaged his post-World War II position which argued that even if one found a totalitarian regime in the world, this fact did not necessarily justify a war, hot or cold, with it. Lippmann's example is also a reminder that the guidelines of "national security" do not of themselves dictate whether to go to war. Lippmann agreed with William Henry Chamberlin by the late 1930s that considerations of national security alone ought to decide American policy. But while Chamberlin saw no German threat, Lippmann discerned one. Lippmann supported American intervention when World War II broke out; Chamberlin supported American noninvolvement. Both agreed at the same time on the evil moral threat posed by totalitarian dictatorships of Left or Right to traditional

---

[37] "Rough-Hew Them How We Will," *Foreign Affairs* 15 (July 1937):594.
[38] "The Economic Consequences of a German Victory," *Life* 9 (July 22, 1940):68.
[39] "The Atlantic and America," *Life* 10 (April 7, 1941):86.

Western civilization, and both were wary of the increased scope assigned to the federal government by the New Deal.

CULTURE AND COMMITMENT: JOSEPH WOOD KRUTCH

It may seem odd to include a man of letters in this collection of sketches devoted to men primarily concerned with public affairs. It is true that Joseph Wood Krutch (1893–1970), drama critic, literary scholar, philosophical essayist, book reviewer, and professor of English at Columbia, was less politically oriented than William Henry Chamberlin, Sidney Hook, and Walter Lippmann. But through Krutch's more literary preoccupation can be seen another dimension of the impact of European totalitarianism on the social thought of American intellectuals in the twentieth century.

Born and raised in Knoxville, Tennessee, Krutch received his undergraduate education at the University of Tennessee. Moving to New York City when he was twenty-one in order to do graduate work in English at Columbia, he became during the 1920s a leading representative of sophisticated New York intellectuals' thought. He covered the Scopes trial in Dayton for *The Nation*, and was complimented by an angry editorial in the *Knoxville Sentinel* attacking his apostasy from Tennessee entitled "We Are Not Proud of Him." Absorbing contemporary psychoanalytic thought, Krutch wrote a psychological interpretation of Edgar Allan Poe. As drama critic for *The Nation* during most of the postwar decade, he sympathetically introduced to readers much of the new theater. Krutch has observed in his autobiography, *More Lives Than One*, of his friends and himself during the early and middle 1920s:

> We were at bottom fundamentally optimistic; and we were gay crusaders. . . . More conspicuously in protestant and satiric literature, but to a considerable extent in social and political criticism also, the most threatening enemies were then not Capitalism, Race Prejudice, or the neglect of the Undeveloped Countries, but Puritanism, Provincialism, and the Genteel Tradition.[40]

Toward the end of the decade Krutch began to question the legitimacy of this optimism, and out of this questioning came his most famous book, *The Modern Temper*, published in 1929. A parallel in many ways to Lippmann's *A Preface to Morals*, *The Modern Temper* explored the

---

[40] Joseph Wood Krutch, *More Lives Than One* (New York: Sloane, 1962), pp. 172, 173. Biographical information not otherwise documented is from the autobiography.

intellectual destruction wrought by modern science, skepticism, and relativism. But while Lippmann at the same time enunciated hope that a new ethical orientation would soon fill the vacuum created by science, even though he could not indicate what the new ethics would be, Krutch agreed with the need for a sense of values but expressed no hope for the emergence of a genuine or valid morality. It was Krutch's basic argument that modern knowledge had rendered man's traditional beliefs or myths incredible. Man had to believe in myths, defined as values or ideas which explained the meaning of life, but man had to believe that the myths were in fact true. Myths which were acknowledged to be false no longer served any purpose. "Standards are imaginary things, and yet it is extremely doubtful if man can live well, either spiritually or physically, without the belief that they are somehow real," he wrote in *The Modern Temper*. "Yet, as that systematized and cumulative experience which is called science displaces one after another the myths which have been generated by need, it grows more and more likely that he must remain an ethical animal in a universe which contains no ethical element." If Krutch's despair was not as pervasive in the 1920s as historians have customarily suggested, it was admittedly not uncommon. And among literary men of the time it was, not rare to make Krutch's distinction between primitive vitality and civilized sterility. As a part of his overall treatment of the debilitation caused by scientific knowledge, he argued that civilizations declined at their moments of greatest learning and culture, to be replaced by more vigorous, confident barbarians. It was a romantic cry of impending doom for Western civilization, but it implied that there were vital life values somewhere, if only among barbarians.

Krutch fused his romantic primitivism with his observations concerning the Soviet Union, following a trip to Russia while he was writing *The Modern Temper*. Although he was by no means sympathetic to the Communists, he interpreted the Bolsheviks as the barbarian wave of the future. He argued in the last chapter of *The Modern Temper* that "there has already developed in Russia a new philosophy of life" which was "essentially primitive in its simplicity." Whereas traditional Western societies concerned themselves with the psychology of the individual and the spiritual relation of man to the universe, "Communism assumes that nothing is really important except those things upon which the welfare of the race depends, and in assuming that it is assuming exactly what a primitive society always assumes." Thus he imputed to the Soviet Union, just as did William Henry Chamberlin and Sidney Hook in the 1920s, a vitality and a place in the future which were not attributed to the United States of America. In the depths of Krutch's pessimism in 1929 there was a curious optimistic strain of romantic primitivism:

If Russia or the Russian spirit conquers Europe it will not be with the bomb of the anarchist but with the vitality of the young barbarian who may destroy many things but who destroys them only that he may begin over again. Such calamities are calamitous only from the point of view of a humanism which values the complexity of its feelings and the subtlety of its intellect far more than nature does. To her they are merely the reassertion of her right to recapture her own world, merely the process by which she repeoples the earth with creatures simple enough to live joyously there.[41]

It is impossible to read such a passage without realizing that the relativistic naturalism upon which it is based could furnish the logic justifying Communist liquidation of class enemies following the Revolution. "Skepticism has entered too deeply into our souls ever to be replaced by faith, and we can never forget the things which the new barbarians will never need to have known," wrote Krutch. "The world may be rejuvenated in one way or another, but we will not."[42] The point is not that Krutch would have defended, even inadvertently, Bolshevik elimination of class enemies. Rather the point is that the same relativistic framework was being used in Sidney Hook's revolutionary defense of Russian violence and Krutch's naturalistic interpretation of history.

Out of a relativism grounded in scientific naturalism, it is psychologically, if not logically, possible to develop a new concern for humane values, and Krutch made this development in the early 1930s. After having demonstrated in *The Modern Temper* that man's values were not real in a scientific or natural sense, Krutch in *Experience and Art* (1932) repeated that whatever meaning man found in the world was meaning he had put there. But he went on to argue for the first time that precisely because of that fact it deserved to be celebrated rather than deprecated. Krutch remained within the naturalistic assumptions of *The Modern Temper*, but in *Experience and Art* he affirmed the worth of esthetic creation and appreciation outside natural reality. It was not until the Soviet dictatorship had attracted such widespread support in the 1930s among American intellectuals, particularly among Krutch's friends on *The Nation* staff, that he was provoked to abandon the naturalistic relativism of *The Modern Temper* and to defend traditional European civilization as being of absolute value. Krutch later recalled that at the beginning of the 1930s he assumed that *The Nation* and most of his friends would remain,

[41] Joseph Wood Krutch, *The Modern Temper* (New York: Harcourt, 1929), pp. 9, 10, 163–164, 166–167.

[42] Krutch, *The Modern Temper*, p. 167.

as they had always been, "libertarian" in their concern for the protection of civil liberties. But gradually he became aware that sympathy for revolutionary communism had led many of his friends to justify dictatorial suppression of civil liberties in the Soviet Union on the grounds that the ends justified the means. The tendency of Krutch's own thought at the time was suggested by his unsigned editorial in *The Nation* of May 3, 1933, commenting on the Soviet trial and conviction of several Russian engineers. He wrote that "it is difficult to see how liberals who have always protested against the effect of class prejudice in other famous cases, who have always pretended, at least, that they demanded a rigidly impartial trial, can logically acquiesce in the methods of Russia just because these liberals happen to sympathize somewhat with the basic aspirations of the Russian people."[43] Krutch has recalled that this editorial marked the opening of an ideological conflict on *The Nation* in which he was opposed by younger radicals who shared his antipathy for fascism but who were more sympathetic to the Soviet Union.

In 1934, in a series of articles entitled "Was Europe a Success?", Krutch directly criticized sympathizers with the Soviet Union who were attempting to revolutionize traditional society. By so doing, he confronted and criticized his own former naturalistic relativism as well. The essays were based on an assumption that the future of European man, or the European heritage, or traditional Europe, was at issue in the demands for change made by contemporary radicals. Whatever the origins of individual criticisms of the existing order, he argued, the ultimate result of revolution was going to be the destruction of traditional European values. Consequently, according to Krutch, it was necessary to assess the past success of Europe in order to know one's attitude toward the desirability of revolution. His conclusion was that only by historical comparison could Europe be called a success, since all its triumphs of law, order, art, learning, and manners were accompanied by brutality, suffering, and class discrimination. Worse than that, Krutch admitted that some of the victories, such as the drama of Shakespeare or Racine, would not have been the same without accompanying defects, such as military pride and the national spirit. "You could not, for example, have Dante without his bigotry," wrote Krutch, "just as you could not—then, at least—have had Plato without the slaves who supported his society."[44] Nevertheless, Krutch's concern was that of distinguishing the various essential and inessential qualities of the European man, and of ascertaining whether the essential

---

[43] "Class Justice," *The Nation* 136 (May 3, 1933):490.

[44] "Was Europe a Success? II. The Question Considered," *The Nation* 139 (August 22, 1934):210.

ones justified the preservation of Europe and the rejection of revolution.

Krutch concluded that the essential attributes of European man were his ideas of personal freedom, the sanctity of the individual, and the possibility of intellectual detachment. Without these beliefs or values, according to Krutch, a man would not be a civilized European. Krutch envisioned the end of these fundamental aspects of European civilization in any Communist society, and he suggested that contemporary Communists even in the United States had taken a fateful step away from essential traditional virtues which Krutch clearly cherished. He said, referring to "most radical radicals":

> both their thinking and their writing certainly lack all those secondary virtues which are commonly implied when we speak of anything or anyone as "civilized." The thinking and the writing are dogmatic, harsh, and intolerant. They are full of an intense and burning hatred for that urbanity, detachment, and sense of fair play which make thinking amiable and which liberals pretend, at least, to admire.
>
> When we have gone this far we may go one step further and wonder if these "secondary virtues" are really secondary; if, in the last analysis, it is possible to be really right without them.[45]

At this point in Krutch's defense of traditional European ideals, he merged his indictment of revolutionary Communists into a joint indictment of Communists and Fascists. "The two parties have arrived at what are usually thought of as diametrically opposed conclusions by mental processes very similar," he wrote, "and it may be suggested as a possibility that the most important, the most fundamental thing is rather the manner or the temper than the conclusions themselves."[46] Thus had Krutch, from a basically literary or cultural perspective, arrived at the same time at the same position as had Walter Lippmann from a more political perspective: an affirmation of the traditional liberal society in the West and in America.

These sketches of the social thought of Chamberlin, Hook, Lippmann, and Krutch during the 1920s and 1930s have emphasized the emergence of an idea of totalitarianism. The common features of the

---

[45] "Was Europe a Success? IV. Some Doubts Arrived At (con't)," *The Nation* 139 (Sept. 5, 1934):267.

[46] "Was Europe a Success? IV.," p. 267.

revolutionary dictatorships, whether of Right or Left, were seen to far
outweigh the differences. Both communism and fascism were viewed as
varieties of the same thing.

For virtually all American intellectuals, Hitler's National Socialism
was so far beyond the pale of moral respectability as never to elicit a
serious defense and hence never to occasion any disillusionment or recon-
sideration. Mussolini's regime aside, for it was briefly the object of attraction in the 1920s for some intellectuals who admired the avowed planning
in corporatism, Fascist countries were always regarded as forces of evil by
American intellectuals. Fascism was customarily regarded as being on the
Right, which was bad, as opposed to the forces of good, which were
located somewhere on the Left. Consequently the perception of Hitler's
rule by American intellectuals was simply the confirmation of what they
already knew concerning the inhumanity and immorality of the Right.
There was no American disillusionment with European fascism, Mussolini
partially excepted, because there had been few illusions. This is not to
deny that Hitler's concentration camps and later his extermination of the
Jews exceeded any inhumanity earlier conceived possible by Americans,
and thus constituted additional evidence to undermine a progressive view
of the world. Nor is it to deny the obviously crucial importance of increasingly anti-Nazi sentiment in drawing the United States to the side of the
Allies prior to Pearl Harbor. But in terms of long-range social thought, the
point is this: the evils of naziism were increasingly regarded by American
intellectuals as not peculiar to Germany but instead as part of a widespread totalitarianism. True, Germany and not the Soviet Union was
viewed as posing the greatest immediate threat to American interests,
ideals, and associations. But to most American intellectuals Nazi Germany had from Hitler's accession to power in 1933 been an evil force,
and the categorization of Germany as one of several totalitarian regimes
or societies caused no rearrangement of the American intellectuals' perception of political and social reality. On the other hand, the merging of
communism with fascism was of enormous intellectual significance.
Communism was assumed even by most early American critics to be at
worst muddleheaded, utopian, otherworldly, too idealistic. Those who
were sympathetic to it saw Bolsheviks as Russian progressives, heirs of
the Enlightenment pointing toward a glorious future. No matter how bad
the Fascists might be, the picture of political and social reality in the mind
of the American intellectual was not basically rearranged until the Communists were seen as guilty of the same sins as the Fascists, which is to
say until the concept of totalitarianism linked them together. However evil
the Fascists, the progressive and pragmatic view of a William Henry
Chamberlin in the 1920s could still prevail as long as hope could still be
placed in the Soviet Union. But if the Soviet Union shared the essential

characteristics of Nazi Germany, which is precisely what the idea of totalitarianism increasingly came to mean after the 1930s, the implications were far-reaching. Instead of the familiar world conflict between progressive experimentation and the status quo, the true fight for a moral man had to be against dictatorships of the Left as well as of the Right, on the assumption that both were totalitarian. The old dichotomy was dissolved. Lost in the anti-Fascist rhetoric of the coming of World War II was the fact that the essential intellectual structure had been articulated by the end of the 1930s, if not disseminated among the populace, for a later Cold War with the Soviets.

Chamberlin, Hook, Lippmann, and Krutch enunciated their discovery of totalitarianism with most explicit reference to the Soviet Union, rather than to naziism, not because they thought the Russians were uniquely totalitarian, but because they assumed the totalitarian character of Hitler's Germany. Chamberlain and Hook, among former Communist sympathizers, and Lippmann and Krutch among nonsympathizers, were a few years ahead of many of their fellow intellectuals in their preoccupation with the concept of totalitarianism, defined to include communism as well as fascism. Which is to say that the four reviewed in this chapter were among the leaders in what became by the end of the decade a pervasive preoccupation of the intellectuals. The Nazis' anti-Semitism, persecution of dissidents, and militarism were sufficiently egregious to offset for some time the Soviet Purge Trials in the eyes of many Americans on the Left who wanted to make a distinction between Hitler and Stalin. The end of the dream for most, however, and the victory of the idea of totalitarianism, came in August of 1939 when Stalin betrayed anti-Nazi idealism by signing the nonaggression pact with Hitler. The accompanying and soon-to-be revealed agreement to dismember Poland was interpreted by most Americans as further revelation of a Soviet likeness with naziism. No longer, it was widely felt in retrospect even by many of the long faithful, could Stalin's liquidation of the peasantry, intellectuals, and dissident Party members be justified as necessary means to presumably progressive ends. The ends were by the fall of 1939 viewed widely as little different from those of Hitler's Germany.

As Walter Lippmann's support of, and William Henry Chamberlin's opposition to, American intervention on behalf of the Allies prior to Pearl Harbor clearly show, a belief in the common totalitarian features of communism and fascism did not by itself dictate what position to take concerning a desirable American foreign policy. What it did do was to contribute to a rapprochement between America and its intellectuals. Whatever position one took during the intervention fight, one argued it as a patriot. If it were contended that the United States should not get involved in Europe's wars, it was because America was superior to, or not in need of, or might get contaminated from, Europe. Whether or not one favored increasing domestic political and economic reform, and most intellectuals did, America was no longer advised to look outside its borders for leadership. If it were argued that the United States should intervene in some way on behalf of England and France, it was because American interests and ideals were allegedly at stake.

This rapprochement, crystallized by the intervention controversy between the outbreak of war in Europe in September of 1939 and the Japanese attack at Pearl Harbor in December of 1941, was part of a pervasive reembracement of America by the intellectuals. Historians who had earlier criticized dominant American institutions as vested interests of special interest groups came to praise the social value of those institutions. Novelists who had earlier in their fiction excoriated the selfishness and inhumanity of Americans came to praise the dignity and worth of their countrymen. In scholarship and letters generally a harsh and critical stance toward things American came to be replaced by a softer position of affirmation. A value-free relativism which emphasized that beliefs and practices of any people are not so much good or bad but rather useful or useless—hence they all are relative to their circumstance—came to be replaced by an absolutism which emphasized or at least implied that American beliefs and practices were morally good. It was of little comfort to the relativists to be able to observe that the expression of moral absolutism was a part of the changing climate of opinion, provoked largely by world events, and hence was relative to new circumstances. And the portentous implications for postwar America could hardly have been realized. Yet the outlines for the next two decades of ruling social thought in the United States had already been drawn.

It was crucial for the history of the idea of totalitarianism that the concept of totalitarianism resulting from a fusion of fascism and communism should have been developed simultaneously with the reembracement of America by her intellectuals. For many profound questions concerning modern society, rather than merely forms of government, were suggested by the idea of totalitarianism in the 1930s—the intellectuals' answers to which at the time and later were significantly influenced by their rapprochement with America. If, for example, unprecedented totalitarian dehumanization and thought control could occur in social orders as different as Nazi Germany and Soviet Russia, were all contemporary societies, including the United States, marked by some totalitarian characteristics? If the early twentieth-century progressive view of human nature and history was shown to be naive by the discovery of European totalitarianism, could one trust his fellow man even to make a success of democratic constitutional government in the United States? As historian Richard Reinitz has said, the significance of the idea of totalitarianism rested in showing that social evil can lie in the future, rather than in the past, where the progressives located it. If this is true, perhaps modernization itself, that process to which the progressives by their very name were committed, could lead to increased oppression on an unprecedented scale. Searching questions and doubts such as these were not pursued by the intellectuals as they should have been in the 1930s and afterwards because of most intellectuals' tendency to celebrate America and the virtues of democratic constitutionalism. The radically disturbing questions which were opened up by the idea of totalitarianism in the 1930s and 1940s were explored far enough to alter significantly the course of social thought in the United States. But the exploration generally stopped at the point at which a more probing analysis of American life might have begun. In short, the reembracement of America by the intellectuals caused the discussion of totalitarianism to be almost exclusively in terms of "them" and "us," featuring comparisons of political and economic systems, rather than a discussion of the full range of the conditions of modern life shared by all peoples in the postindustrial world.

4

PROGRESSIVISM IN ECLIPSE: A NEW CONSERVATISM IN THE 1940s AND 1950s

The conservative implications of the idea of European totalitarianism were not immediately evident to most intellectuals in the 1930s. It is true that radicals on the Left were acutely aware that the idea was being used to discredit their plans for reconstructing society by categorizing them together with Fascists. But as World War II approached, and finally erupted in the fall of 1939 simultaneously with the Nazi-Soviet pact and the climax of the idea of European totalitarianism, America was threatened by Fascists and not by Communists. Particularly after Germany broke the pact and attacked Russia in the spring of 1941, and after the Japanese bombing of Pearl Harbor in December of the same year, Americans became preoccupied with Fascist totalitarianism. The Soviets were Allies after 1941, and the idea of totalitarianism that joined Fascists with Communists receded into the background.

It was not simply that Americans forgot what they had increasingly insisted prior to 1941—that the Soviet Union was as totalitarian as Nazi Germany—but rather that enthusiasm for the Allied war effort and Russian cooperation generally took precedence. And of course partnership with the Soviets during the war offered an opportunity to those who had been earlier sympathetic to the Communist experiment to recapture at least some of their prior sympathy and to lay stress upon Bolshevik virtues. The editors of New Republic, for example, had only with great reluctance abandoned their admiration for the Russians and had regretfully concluded at the end of the 1930s that the Soviets were totalitarian. The German invasion of Russia in June of 1941 became almost as important a turning point to New Republic editors as the Nazi-Soviet pact in August of 1939 had been in the opposite direction. Stalin became not merely a heroic ally after 1941, but sometimes seemed in the New Republic to recapture his Old Left figure as humanitarian leader of Russian social democracy. It was a mixed picture in which the New Republic editorials and articles sometimes argued simply for pragmatic war support of the Communists, and on other occasions argued that the Soviet Union was in some meaningful sense moving toward democracy and a peaceful foreign policy.[1] In either case, the idea of a Soviet totalitarianism which could be equated with Fascist totalitarianism was minimized, if not actually denied.

Such old-time anti-Communists as the editors of the Saturday Evening Post did not stop reminding readers that Russians were imprisoned by the same totalitarianism as were the Germans.[2] But as the war progressed, editorials in the Post increasingly emphasized that the Soviet Union was bravely fighting for the same reason as the United States, because her territory was attacked, that cooperation was necessary and possible between different political systems, and that Stalin was best understood as a practical statesman rather than an ideological revolutionary.[3] Life magazine presented a more simplified version of the same position. Pictures and articles accented Russian heroism in a death struggle with German troops, and reported the willingness of Americans to cooperate with the Soviets in the war effort.[4] At the same time readers were occasionally reminded that the Communist regime was a dictatorship which contradicted democratic ideals.[5]

---

[1] For examples of practical support, see New Republic 104 (June 30, 1941):871–872; 105 (October 13, 1941):454–455; 109 (August 30, 1943):267–268; 110 (March 27, 1944):395–396. For examples of ideological support, see New Republic 105 (July 7, 1941):17–18; 107 (December 21, 1942):811–812; 108 (April 5, 1943):433–437; 110 (January 31, 1944):132.

[2] See Saturday Evening Post 214 (November 8, 1941):26; 214 (March 21, 1942):26; 216 (September 18, 1943):116; 217 (August 12, 1944):100.

[3] See Saturday Evening Post 215 (July 18, 1942):88; 215 (December 12, 1942):116; 216 (August 28, 1943):100; 217 (August 12, 1944):100.

[4] See Life 11 (July 28, 1941):17–19; 13 (July 27, 1942):30–31; 14 (April 19, 1943):30; 16 (January 31, 1944):24.

[5] See Life 14 (March 29, 1943):20; 14 (May 10, 1943):30; 15 (December 20, 1943):32; 19 (July 30, 1945):20.

The hiatus of the war years aside, it nonetheless remains a fact that the 1930s brought a prefiguration of the social thought that would emerge dominant after the Axis powers were defeated. The new directions charted during the depression decade by such men as William Henry Chamberlin, Sidney Hook, Walter Lippmann, and Joseph Wood Krutch would be pursued by most Americans in the late 1940s and 1950s. The guidelines would structure the rationale for America's role in the Cold War and for an essentially conservative postwar domestic political temper.

ISOLATIONIST TO COLD WARRIOR: WILLIAM HENRY CHAMBERLIN, III

The pervasive influence of the wartime cooperation with the Russians left its mark even upon one so anti-Soviet as William Henry Chamberlin. Early infatuated with the Bolshevik experiment in the 1920s, early disillusioned with Stalin in the 1930s, and one of the first Americans to dwell on the existence of a Communist totalitarianism which was virtually identical with that of Nazi Germany, Chamberlin advocated in 1940 an isolationist foreign policy for the United States.

Like other vehement prewar critics of the Soviet Union, Chamberlin did not during the war explicitly take back any of his previous criticisms of Stalin's totalitarianism. But they were soft-pedaled in favor of an emphasis upon Russian characteristics which contributed to the Allied war effort, suggested continuity with traditional Tsarist Russia rather than revolutionary bolshevism, and which held out hope for peaceful cooperation in the postwar world. Joseph Stalin was portrayed in *The Russian Enigma* in 1943 as "a shrewd, hard-headed realist, without any paranoid delusions of grandeur." Chamberlin wrote of Stalin:

> If he must bear responsibility for many acts of ruthless cruelty against individuals and classes that stood in the way of his plans, he must also, in fairness, be given credit for the great industrial and military progress which the Soviet Union achieved during this time. If he liquidated the Kulaks, he built Magnitogorsk, the big new iron and steel centre in the Southern Urals, together with scores of other plants equipped to turn out machinery, tractors and chemicals. If he carried his blood-feud with the Old Bolsheviks to a bitter and tragic end, he built up a military machinery that could hit back with strength and success after standing up to the fiercest mechanized onslaughts of Hitler's streamlined legions.[6]

Communist theory mattered little to Stalin, who "may reasonably be expected to do at any given moment what seems to serve his own interests,

---

[6] W. H. Chamberlin, *The Russian Enigma* (New York: Scribner, 1943), pp. 119, 120.

and Russia's, most effectively, quite irrespective of doctrinaire consistency."

The implications for Soviet foreign policy of Stalin's flexibility included a willingness on the part of the Communist leader to do whatever was necessary to protect Russian security, regardless of Marxist-Leninist doctrine. "Russia First" was Stalin's rule, and a "demonic interpretation" of the Soviets as fomenters of international revolution no longer fit the facts, according to Chamberlin. "A desire to be let alone may not be the last word in international virtue and wisdom," he wrote. "But it is much to be preferred to a spirit of restless predatory imperialism."

Nationalism had replaced social revolution as the guiding theme of the Soviets. "The proletarian revolutionary note has simply dropped out of the Soviet propaganda chorus." Partly caused by the increasing conservatism of the Russian regime, the spirit of nationalism was also the result of the war. And a further effect of the war would likely be a postwar loosening of the dictatorship. "It is at least a strong possibility that the Russian people after the war will not be so submissive to the arbitrary rule of the political police," wrote Chamberlin, "will not allow themselves to be forced back into that mold of tight one-party dictatorship which the war itself has broken to some extent."[7] One need only remember Chamberlin's earlier pacifism, his fear of wartime regimentation, and his earlier interpretation of the inflexibility of Soviet totalitarianism to realize the extent to which these passages from *The Russian Enigma* in 1943 reflected the climate of the Allied war effort.

As Allied victory drew near, however, Chamberlin returned to his prewar emphasis upon Soviet totalitarianism. "Here is a war that is supposedly being fought against totalitarianism," he wrote in early 1945 in *America: Partner in World Rule*, but "it has made the first of the totalitarian states, the Soviet Union, the strongest land power in Europe and Asia." This irony was reiterated in much of Chamberlin's postwar writing on American foreign policy, and he was increasingly critical of the United States for its part in Russia's growth to world power. He blamed Franklin Roosevelt for allying America to Great Britain through economic and military assistance prior to Pearl Harbor, and for provoking the Japanese attack by cutting off economic assistance. Chamberlin thought neither policy was required to protect the security of the United States. Americans misconceived World War II as a conflict between the British and the Germans, whereas in truth it was a struggle between Hitler and Stalin. The consequence of Roosevelt's actions was to secure the victory of one totalitarian regime over another. And just as Woodrow Wilson's proposed Fourteen Points for peace bore little relation to what happened following World War I, Winston Churchill's and Franklin Roosevelt's idealistic At-

---

[7] Chamberlin, *The Russian Enigma*, pp. 133, 205, 271, 289.

lantic Charter guidelines of August 1941 were certain to be violated in the postwar world. Eastern Europe would be the victim of Soviet aggrandizement, in contradiction to the principle of self-determination and self-government of peoples. The meaning of the war seemed to Chamberlin in 1945 to be found mainly in the American contribution to a victorious Soviet imperialism.

As Chamberlin returned at the end of the war to his emphasis upon Russian totalitarianism, dictatorial in its politics and collectivist in its economics, he freely admitted that the possibility of American isolation was gone. The United States was necessarily going to be a partner in world rule as a result of World War II. The nature of that partnership could be phrased in terms of liberty and totalitarianism. America's responsibility was to "attempt to restore four freedoms of the nineteenth century which helped to make that century one of remarkable progress and relieved many sources of strain and tension," Chamberlin said in *America: Partner in World Rule*. "These were all freedoms of movement —for men, ideas, goods, and capital."[8] These freedoms would all be opposed by the Russian partners in world rule, however. Dictatorial repression in all areas of life when in power, and revolutionary propaganda and subversion when not in power, would be the Communist practice following the war.

In 1946 Chamberlin edited a collection of historical documents of the Communist International from the 1920s, which reflected his conclusion that the Soviet declaration of a worldwide revolution was not, after all, a dead letter. He justified reprinting the promulgations "which set forth with complete authority and with remarkable detail the technique by means of which Communism hopes to conquer the world" on the grounds that the threat of communism was much greater in 1946 "than it was in 1920 or in 1928, when these blueprints of international conspiracy were composed." As Chamberlin presented these Communist manifestoes to the American public, he argued that they were "the iron dogmas of Communist philosophy," and that "Stalin is just as much committed to the ultimate objective of world revolution through the overthrow of all 'capitalist' States as was Trotsky." In contrast to what Chamberlin had said during the war concerning the possibility of coexistence, he insisted in *Blueprint for World Conquest* that "in Stalin's mind there is irreconcilable hostility between the Soviet Union and the 'capitalist' world." Thus it was not enough for Stalin to have friendly territorial neighbors. To Stalin, "Russia can never know security so long as 'capitalist' (i.e., democratic) States continue to exist."

---

[8] W. H. Chamberlin, *America: Partner in World Rule* (New York: Vanguard, 1945), pp. 52, 288.

Chamberlin had articulated the core of a rationale for a cold or even a hot war between the United States and the Soviet Union. An enemy existed which not only held an unwavering goal of international revolution, but which conceived of its national security in terms so broad as to require the destruction of all different forms of government. The ideological conflict was between Communist totalitarianism and democracy. But the threat was not merely ideological, nor could considerations of national security be defined so as to await military aggression against the United States. The Communist International made clear that the function of Communist parties and sympathizers outside of the Soviet Union was to engage in subversion. "A few Communists, knowing what they want and working closely together, can often infiltrate into key positions in a trade-union, a so-called cultural organization, a government agency," Chamberlin wrote in what amounted to a preamble to loyalty and security investigations which were soon to follow. The Communist International outlined a conspiracy in the 1920s which the Russians were inevitably implementing in the 1940s, according to Chamberlin, and "the only sensible attitude of the United States and other democratic countries toward the blueprint of organized subversion which is outlined in these documents is to maintain the eternal vigilance that in this age, perhaps more than ever, is the price of liberty."[9]

Having fully developed a position by 1946 of hard-line opposition to the Soviets abroad and of warning against Communist subversion at home, Chamberlin was in the vanguard of Cold Warriors. During the late forties he argued with increasing vehemence that Americans had faiied, during the 1930s and again in the war, to understand the concept of totalitarianism as applying equally to communism and fascism. Outlining the characteristics which the Nazis shared in common with the Soviets, Chamberlin declared that Russian militarism, aggression, and imperialism were predictable. Indicative of his increasing dogmatism was Chamberlin's willingness to read the minds of Soviet leaders. Whereas he had entitled one of his books published as recently as 1943 *The Russian Enigma*, and had devoted the first chapter to a discussion of "Why Russia Is an Enigma," Chamberlin was confident by the late 1940s that he had penetrated the puzzle. "A good deal of nonsense has been written about the Soviet regime as a riddle, a mystery, an enigma, and what not," Chamberlin wrote in *America's Second Crusade* in 1950, but "there is no secret about the underlying philosophy of communism." The Communist International had announced its aim of worldwide revolution in the 1920s and Stalin was inflexibly committed to it in the 1940s.

---

[9] W. H. Chamberlin, *Blueprint for World Conquest* (Chicago: Human Events, 1946), pp. 1, 2, 8, 10, 23, 27.

Chamberlin laid increasing responsibility for Russia's successes during the 1940s at Franklin Roosevelt's door. By 1950 Chamberlin stated not only that Nazi Germany never threatened American security, but that "German ambitions were directed toward the east, not toward the west." The United States foolishly and unnecessarily went to war on behalf of Great Britain. But Chamberlin went further. "There is no proof that Britain and France would ever have been attacked if they had not gone to war on the Polish issue," he said, and "Britain at any time could have had peace on the basis of retaining its fleet and its empire." What this inescapably meant was that England and France gratuitously declared war on Germany in 1939 on behalf of Poland following her attack by Hitler's armies, and that had England and France not done so, Germany and Russia would have wounded each other, hopefully beyond recovery, in a bloodbath of totalitarian regimes. Given this bright alternative utopia of what might have been, a world without a powerful Stalin or Hitler, Chamberlin cast Roosevelt's policies into even greater darkness. The United States saved the Soviet Union from probable destruction at the hands of the Germans, then appeased Stalin by giving him eastern Europe. "We do not know, and perhaps never shall know, how much outright treason was mingled with stupidity, opportunism, emotional fellow-traveler admiration of the Soviet regime, and sheer ignorance in shaping American wartime attitudes and activities," Chamberlin wrote in the spring of 1950, shortly after Senator Joseph McCarthy's initial charges of Communist subversion in the government.[10]

During the 1950s Chamberlin became more self-conscious concerning the conservative implications of the direction of his thought ever since his Depression disillusionment with communism, and he called an autobiographical volume published at the end of the decade *The Evolution of a Conservative*. Citing the thought of Edmund Burke, *The Federalist*, John Adams, Alexis de Tocqueville, John C. Calhoun, and Jacob Burkhardt, Chamberlin wrote that as he "became more familiar with the classics of conservative thought" he "became increasingly convinced that this was my faith."[11] As his autobiographical testament made clear, however, it was a conservatism defined largely in terms of nineteenth-century liberalism. His invocation of conservatism revealed the ambiguities which Allen Guttmann in *The Conservative Tradition in America* has said characterized much of the "new conservatism" of the 1950s: it frequently celebrated Burke's insistence upon tradition and evolutionary change, on

---

[10] W. H. Chamberlin, *America's Second Crusade* (Chicago: Regnery, 1950), pp. 38, 93, 256.

[11] W. H. Chamberlin, *The Evolution of a Conservative* (Chicago: Regnery, 1959), p. 74.

the one hand, but on the other, often refused to accept changes which had occurred in the twentieth century and asked for a return to earlier laissez-faire policies.[12] Chamberlin likened his own criticisms of the revolutionary changes brought by the Bolsheviks to Burke's opposition to the French Revolution, and he articulated the Burkean "conservative distrust of change for the sake of change and of schemes for reshaping society in line with doctrinaire blueprints." Chamberlin emphasized too the imperfectibility of man, the importance of religious and patriotic traditions, and the potential danger of democratic rule. But he placed equal stress upon the need for a return to economic individualism and a weaker federal government (except in foreign affairs), and the validity of the Horatio Alger myth as a fact in the past and as a model for the future. Herbert Hoover and Robert Taft were singled out as ideal conservatives.

Chamberlin did not easily accept the conditions of life in the United States which had evolved by the 1950s. Instead he often voiced a strong jeremiad, marking the decline of America from the 1800s, and pleading for a return to the earlier golden age. The welfare state taxed the able to reward the unfit, progressive education reflected a degenerate social permissiveness, and a loose sentimentalism failed to cope with a rising crime rate and the failure of Negroes to perform on an equal level with whites. Consistent with his indictment of the American failure to perpetuate an alleged earlier individualism, and instead to support a welfare state, Chamberlin declared that the twentieth century had brought a "decline in the sense of individual moral responsibility."[13] Such criticisms as these of contemporary American life in 1959 filled a chapter entitled "What's Wrong with America." No more revealing indication could be made of Chamberlin's political perspective than to observe the lack of any reference to the existence of poverty, the disfranchisement of Negroes in the South, and the generally disadvantaged position of ethnic minorities in the United States. For William Henry Chamberlin the psychology, if not the logic, of the discovery of European totalitarianism was conservative in its implications for his view of American society.

LIBERTY AND AUTHORITY IN AN AGE OF TOTALITARIANISM: SIDNEY HOOK, II

William Henry Chamberlin's plea in 1946 that communism be recognized as a unified underground revolutionary movement around the world, and that American Communists be exposed, was to be loudly answered in the rise of what became known as "McCarthyism," the Big

---

[12] Allen Guttmann, *The Conservative Tradition in America* (New York: Oxford, 1967), Chap. VI.

[13] Chamberlin, *The Evolution of a Conservative*, pp. 15, 112.

Red Scare of the Cold War years. The most obvious causes of the hysteria over communism were the revelations that members of the Communist party occupied positions in the federal government during the Roosevelt years and committed some acts of espionage, however rare and insignificant; the partisan desire among Republicans to find an issue that could help win the presidency in 1952 after twenty years of Democratic control of the White House; the frustration, felt first in the late 1940s, over the fact that not peace but a Cold War had followed the termination of World War II, and second and more intensely, frustration felt between 1950 and 1953 over the prolonged stalemate of the Korean War.

The Alger Hiss case was the beginning, on the national level, of the postwar preoccupation with internal Communist subversion. In 1948, Whittaker Chambers, an editor of *Time* magazine and an ex-Communist, accused Hiss, graduate of Harvard Law School, one-time legal secretary to Justice Oliver Wendell Holmes, minor member of Roosevelt's New Deal administration and one of the staff at Yalta, of being a member of the Communist party from 1934 to 1938. Further, according to Chambers, Hiss was part of an espionage ring, took secret government documents to copy and to pass on to the Soviets through Chambers. Hiss denied the accusations but, partly due to the efforts of a young Congressman from California, Richard Nixon, Hiss was indicted for perjury. In January of 1950, after the first trial resulted in a hung jury, Hiss was convicted of two counts of perjury, including his denial that he passed secret documents to Chambers.

The case was a sensation, even before Whittaker Chambers reached into a hollowed pumpkin on his farm to get some of the microfilmed documents which he said Hiss had copied in 1938. It was sensational to charge Communist subversion against a respected government servant who moved in the circles of American leadership. Secretary of State Acheson, Governor Adlai Stevenson of Illinois, and Justice Felix Frankfurter all publicly vouched for Hiss's character. Yet, despite his denial of guilt and the continued support of a considerable number of people, most who followed the case probably agreed with the second jury that Alger Hiss had been a Communist and had passed secrets to the Soviets.

The month following the Hiss conviction, it was announced by the British government that Dr. Klaus Fuchs, a physicist, had confessed that he passed scientific secrets to the Russians from 1943 to 1947 while he was engaged in atomic research in the United States and in England. In March of 1950 Fuchs was convicted. In May of 1950 Harry Gold, a hospital chemist in Philadelphia, was arrested on the basis of a voluntary confession that he had been the courier in the United States in 1944–1945 between Klaus Fuchs and a Russian vice-consul. In June 1950 David Greenglass, a machinist who as a soldier had been stationed at Los

Alamos Atomic Project, was arrested for having been an accomplice of Harry Gold in 1945. In July 1950 Julius Rosenberg, owner of a small machine shop in New York City and brother-in-law of David Greenglass, was arrested on charges of having conspired to commit espionage with Greenglass and Gold in 1944–1945. In August of 1950 Ethel, wife of Julius Rosenberg and sister of David Greenglass, was arrested on the same charge.

These shocking events, in addition to Cold War frustrations and Republican party opportunism, surrounded the emergence of Senator Joseph McCarthy's famous Communist witch-hunt. Launching his attack in February of 1950 before the Women's Republican Club in Wheeling, West Virginia, the junior Wisconsin Senator waved a piece of paper which he claimed contained the names of 205 Communists in the State Department. The number of names thereafter declined when McCarthy repeated the allegations around the country and in the Senate. A Senate investigating committee, headed by conservative Democrat Millard Tydings, found McCarthy's charges baseless, but McCarthy pressed his attack forward, accusing the Democrats of selling out America to the Communists for twenty years. Republicans, hungry for election victories, hesitated to criticize McCarthy. Democrats, fearful that the Republicans might gain a monopoly of the "Communists in government" issue, began to join in the witch-hunt. The politicians assumed that the consequences of opposing McCarthy were politically dangerous. The voters were thought to be sympathetic to McCarthy, and he was considered vindictive and unscrupulous. When Senator Tydings ran for reelection in the fall of 1950, McCarthy contributed to his defeat by supplying doctored photographs portraying Tydings with Communists.

In September of 1950 the Democratic-controlled Congress passed, over President Truman's veto, an Internal Security Act which required Communist organizations to publish their records, though it did not outlaw their organizations; it authorized punishment of Communists who advocated totalitarian dictatorship in the United States; it barred Communists from employment in defense plants and from obtaining passports; and it established the Subversive Activities Control Board to help expose Communists. Following General Eisenhower's election in 1952 and the accompanying Republican control of Congress, McCarthy became chairman of the Government Operations Committee and its Permanent Subcommittee on Investigations. In 1953 and 1954 he led investigative attacks concerning alleged Communist influence in the Voice of America, American libraries overseas, the Central Intelligence Agency, and the United States Army. William Henry Chamberlin's plea had indeed been more than answered.

The history of American social thought during the postwar years is not to be found in the facts of the spy trials nor even in the activities of Senator McCarthy and other Red hunters, but in the reaction to them. Virtually no Americans defended Communist subversion, and few intellectuals defended the tactics of a McCarthy. The question was how one interpreted the facts of Communist subversion and McCarthyism. This question itself was illustrative of the postwar climate of opinion. It represented a shift in the focus of social thought from an early twentieth-century and Great Depression debate over the existence and solution of economic, political, and social problems, to a postwar debate over the legal and moral implications and relations of individual liberty and state authority in a free society threatened by totalitarianism. The character of social thought at any time is marked for the historian as much by its general preoccupations as by its specific proposals. During the Depression, for New Dealers or radicals, the primary focus was upon finding solutions for economic problems determined to be critically serious, and relatively little attention was paid to constitutional or legal problems. During the late 1940s and 1950s, however, the priorities were reversed due to the perception of a threat to national security by a totalitarian force which was specifically defined in terms of its opposition to democratic constitutional process. The United States became the defender of democratic constitutionalism, and the protection of minorities and civil liberties within it. The alleged commitment of Communist totalitarianism to worldwide revolutionary activity made an immediately practical problem of what might have been merely an ideological one. Americans insisted that what fundamentally distinguished their system of government from a totalitarian regime was the dignity accorded a human being, the freedom granted any individual, and the protection offered a dissenting minority. Yet Americans increasingly defined communism not only as totalitarian but as bent upon the destruction of any democratic system. Consequently, if one accepted this interpretation, dissent was not wholly from within but also from without, not wholly nor perhaps even a part of the democratic constitutional system but instead an attack upon it. To this problem of delimiting individual liberty in an America threatened by communism, Sidney Hook devoted much of his tireless writing and lecturing after World War II.

Hook did not intend to turn his back on the experimental method when he discovered totalitarianism and rejected the revolutionary radicalism of his youth. In 1943 he attacked "The New Failure of Nerve" on the part of those who were turning away from a pragmatic or scientific approach in favor of more traditional or religious perspectives. "There is hardly a field of theoretical life from which these signs of intellectual panic, heralded as portents of spiritual revival, are lacking," Hook wrote. "The attack upon scientific method, in order to be free to believe whatever voice speaks to us, is a flight from responsibility." He admitted that the reasons for a widespread failure of nerve stemmed from the tragic destruction of men's hopes in the twentieth century, but he denied that this tragedy was due to the scientific spirit. "The truth is that scientific method has until now been regarded as irrelevant in testing the values embodied in social institutions."[14] Hook had been persistent for almost half a century in pleading for a pragmatic attitude toward life. But it is doubtful whether his experimentalism explains much about why his social thought developed as it did. When he was a youthful revolutionary theorist, he interpreted Marx according to John Dewey and made Marx a pragmatic Communist. After World War II, Hook continued to emphasize the scientific temper. In fact, he interpreted democratic constitutionalism as a kind of pragmatic method of investigating social and political issues. As the pragmatic method set up guidelines for the discussion of beliefs of policies, so democratic constitutionalism created a structure for nonviolent resolution of differences. As the pragmatic method vitiated abstract absolutes and incorporated human considerations into its discussion, yet did not specify a standard of judgment, so democratic constitutionalism was by, for, and of the people, yet did not stipulate substantive answers to problems. Hook interpreted democratic constitutionalism pragmatically, just as he had interpreted communism pragmatically. His rhetoric of experimentalism remained constant; his substantive social views changed dramatically.

The youthful Sidney Hook was a Marxist activist who tried to furnish a rationale for revolutionary communism. That he could justify in theory liquidation of class enemies in a Communist revolution was a measure of his commitment. But the failure of the Soviet Union to implement theory turned Hook not only against Russian practice but against revolutionary theory as well. By the late 1930s Hook had altered his earlier radical "capitalist" versus "communist" conflict to a new mortal combat between "totalitarianism" and "democracy." It would be hard to overstate the importance of the idea of totalitarianism for Hook's postwar social thought. When he discussed academic freedom, the meaning of invoking the Fifth Amendment, and national security, he always argued from the perspective of an absolute, unchanging chasm separating democracy and totalitarianism, the United States and the Soviet Union. The same stark distinction between good and evil which allowed the young radical Hook to issue a theoretical justification for the liquidation of class enemies led Hook after World War II to categorize and damn Communists and communism.

---

[14] "The New Failure of Nerve," *Partisan Review* 10 (January–February 1943):2, 8, 10.

Consistent with Hook's basic distinction between democracy and totalitarianism was his fundamental dichotomy dividing kinds of protest or dissent leveled against the American status quo. "Heresy" was dissent expressed openly within the legal channels, and he declared it essential to the vitality of a democratic society, in *Heresy, Yes—Conspiracy, No,* published in 1953. He defined "conspiracy," by contrast, as a "secret or underground movement which seeks to attain its ends not by normal political or educational processes but by playing outside the rules of the game." Dissent in the form of a conspiracy threatened the life of a democracy because it would undemocratically overthrow the society if it could. Heresy was democratic, conspiracy was totalitarian.

Hook attacked both those "cultural vigilantes" on the Right who took heretics to be conspirators and "ritualistic liberals" on the Left who took conspirators to be heretics. "Cultural vigilantes" were "the political demagogues in *both* political parties, religious fundamentalists in both Catholic and Protestant denominations, and some zealots and marginal types in some patriotic organizations," he wrote. "To these must be added certain lobbyists and advertisers who wish to discount the principles of democratic socialism, the New Deal, the Welfare State—the strongest enemies of communism—because the economic and social interests they represent would be adversely affected were these principles widely carried out." Hook, who continued to call himself a socialist, did not follow Chamberlin in translating his opposition to totalitarianism into opposition to the welfare state and to the principles of economic collectivism.

The fact that Hook supported the extension of New Deal measures suggests the complexity of emphasizing the conservatism of postwar social thought. Hook, and others who favored the development of the welfare state in the late 1940s and 1950s, did not think of themselves as conservative. They saw themselves as supporting policies that had formerly been advocated by New Deal reformers and that went beyond what the New Deal had done, which was true. But the same political position does not mean the same thing in different historical contexts. Cold War issues concerning loyalty and security became paramount in the postwar years, and the urgency of old New Deal economic questions was diminished. Insofar as Sidney Hook almost completely emphasized Cold War problems of liberty and authority, and insofar as the positions he took on these problems were designed to support the existing democratic constitutional order, his thought can be characterized as conservative.

The hysteria, public witch-hunt frenzy, and partisan political opportunism associated with the security and loyalty investigations during the late forties and early fifties were excoriated by Hook. But at the same time he attacked those "ritualistic liberals" who acted as if no problem of Communist subversion existed, who ignored "the mass of evidence concerning the conspiratorial character of the Communist movement in all institutions in which it is active." Hook devoted much of his attention to chastising the liberal intellectual community for exaggerating the evils of loyalty and security investigations, and for inviting McCarthyism by failing to support proper national security measures.

Hook lampooned the tens of thousands of "ritualistic liberals" who publicly protested in the 1950s that they and other Americans had been intimidated by McCarthyism. He ridiculed the statement by Robert Hutchins in 1951 that "Everywhere in the U.S. university professors, whether or not they have tenure, are silenced by the general atmosphere of repression that now prevails." Hook retorted that "the facts are that no professor who was in the habit of speaking up five years ago has been silenced, many who were silent five years ago are speaking up, while those who were silent five, ten, fifteen years ago and are still silent cannot be regarded as victims of a reign of terror."[15] Without excusing the Red hunt, Hook implicitly weakened criticism of it by minimizing its significance. Few innocent Americans, he concluded, were really hurt or affected by McCarthyism.

Further at odds with those he called "ritualistic liberals," Hook indicted the use of the Fifth Amendment. During the loyalty and security investigations of the late 1940s and 1950s many persons refused to answer questions concerning their past political activity on the Fifth Amendment ground that such answers might tend to incriminate them. While admitting the legal propriety of the invocation of the Fifth Amendment, Hook criticized those who argued that no inference could be made on the part of the public concerning the guilt of an individual who invoked the Fifth Amendment. Hook insisted, in *Common Sense and the Fifth Amendment*, that its "invocation establishes a presumption of guilt or unfitness *with respect to the issue in question* which is relevant to inferences made in a non-legal or moral context."[16] If one is an ex-Communist or a Communist who did not want to admit his past or present, Hook said, the right not to talk is legally protected—but common sense dictates that observers will draw certain inferences from the failure to respond. Because of the circumstances in which the Fifth Amendment was usually invoked, in front of controversial legislative investigative committees such as McCarthy's, the self-incrimination involved had less to do with criminal prosecution than with public disgrace and possible loss of employment. To some Americans the invocation of the Fifth Amendment was a just ob-

---

[15] Sidney Hook, *Heresy, Yes—Conspiracy, No* (New York: John Day, 1953), pp. 22, 11, 27, 61.

[16] Sidney Hook, *Common Sense and the Fifth Amendment* (New York: Criterion, 1957). Quote appears on page 13 of Regnery edition (Chicago, 1963).

struction to the work of the investigative committees as well as a justifiable privilege for the individual. To Hook the invocation of the Fifth Amendment was tantamount to an admission of guilt. Again, without excusing McCarthyism, Hook undermined criticism of it by his interpretation of the meaning of the invocation of the Fifth Amendment.

Throughout the 1950s Sidney Hook maintained his critique of the Right as well as of the Left, and he denied that he regarded the excesses of the "ritualistic liberals" as any more dangerous than those of the "cultural vigilantes."[17] But it is nonetheless true that the significance of Hook's ideas among intellectuals lay in their attack against the Left. He insisted that government employment, as other employment, was a privilege rather than a right, and that consequently it was proper to deny employment in sensitive areas to citizens who were merely suspected of Communist sympathies. He asserted that Communists did not have open minds and therefore could not pursue academic work in a scholarly fashion, and that Communist teachers should be presumed unfit unless they could prove the contrary. In all these arguments Hook's attack was directed principally at the "ritualistic liberal" who refused to admit the chasm between Communist totalitarianism and democracy, who failed to see that Communists were subversives, and who did not admit that the rise of McCarthyism was understandable even if not justifiable.

ABSOLUTISM AND PRACTICALITY: WALTER LIPPMANN, III

The most significant aspect of Walter Lippmann's social thought during the 1940s and 1950s was the general relation between his traditional and absolutistic ideas and his practical flexibility in the specific area of foreign relations. His more philosophical thought became increasingly conservative, as did the overall climate of opinion in the United States, but his criticisms of America's ideological crusade in the Cold War offered a reminder that a different foreign policy might have been equally compatible with the basically conservative temper of the times.

Lippmann's change of philosophic stance from critical pragmatic progressive to venerable conservator of liberal traditions was already completed before the 1940s. In *The Good Society* in 1937, as discussed in the previous chapter, he fully articulated his defense of traditional democratic constitutionalism and economic individualism. This defense, like Joseph Wood Krutch's at the same time, was given in a spirit of fearful apprehension rather than of triumph, for both Krutch and Lippmann were afraid that the West they admired might be collapsing amid the rise of totalitarian dictatorships.

---

[17] See, for example, *Heresy, Yes—Conspiracy, No.*

The book entitled *Essays in the Public Philosophy* comprised Lippmann's major jeremiad after World War II. He expressed greater pessimism than ever before concerning the ability of the masses to be politically responsible, and for the first time he equated the traditional Western beliefs and policies which he defended with a transcendent body of natural law. Lippmann had been critical before, particularly after World War I, of the intellectual processes of ordinary mortals. But he had never, as he did in the 1950s, charged the democratization of government with bringing about almost everything he disliked in modern political history. So thoroughgoing was his attack on the disastrous influence of public opinion on government that he felt he "should say that I am a liberal democrat and have no wish to disenfranchise my fellow citizens."

Lippmann argued that the increased influence of the mass of men upon public leaders had directly caused the disastrous statesmanship of western Europe countries since World War I, and indirectly caused the rise of totalitarianism. He declared that the "people have acquired power which they are incapable of exercising, and the governments they elect have lost powers which they must recover if they are to govern." The course of the history of the West, he argued, had been downhill since 1914, and it was due to the democratization of government. As public opinion has become an ever-greater force in determining public policies specific decisions have become worse, particularly in the area of foreign relations. The people, Lippmann wrote, "have compelled the governments, which usually knew what would have been wiser, or was necessary, or was more expedient, to be too late with too little, or too long with too much, too pacifist in peace and too bellicose in war, too neutralist or appeasing in negotiation or too intransigent." Thus public opinion made a crusade of World War I and rendered a conciliatory peace impossible. When resentful Germans rebelled against the status quo in the 1930s, public opinion in the West, "recently too warlike to make peace with the unarmed German Republic, had become too pacifist to take the risks which could have prevented the war Hitler was announcing he would wage against Europe." And so the cycle of public opinion's extremism and misjudgment continued through World War II and into the Cold War. As in foreign policy, so in domestic policy, people in the mass have been incurably wrong headed on matters of the public interest. They always prefer the easy to the hard, the pleasant to the painful; they prefer to spend rather than to save, to demand rather than to compromise. "There is then a general tendency to be drawn downward, as by the force of gravity, towards insolvency, towards the insecurity of factionalism, towards the erosion of liberty, and towards hyperbolic wars."

The totalitarian dictatorships, according to Lippmann, provided evidence for his indictment of the democratization of Western government insofar as they recognized the need for effective leadership and power. The "totalitarian counterrevolution," in Lippmann's phrase, was in part a response to the failure of the executive in the liberal democratic state to govern effectively. Paradoxically the same public opinion which crippled effective government would later support a "totalitarian counterrevolution" in order to achieve governmental action. In part, too, totalitarianism in its Communist form represented the ultimate radical democratization of government. Although Lippmann granted that the modern democratic influence could lead to liberal constitutionalism as well as to totalitarianism, he insisted that the former was losing out to the latter. Instead of encouraging people to build a constitutional democracy, the democratic impulse in the twentieth century was leading them to "the revolutionary collision between the inviolable governing caste and the excluded men claiming the redress of their grievances and their place in the sun." The urge toward revolution found its source in the democratic impulse. Revolutionary attackers "declare that evil in society has been imposed upon the many by the few—by priests, nobles, capitalists, imperialists, liberals, aliens—and that evil will disappear when the many who are pure have removed these few who are evil." This utopianism was pervasive in the modern world even where there had not yet been a totalitarian revolution. Public education in democratic societies, Lippmann argued, has become basically ˙a counterpart to a Jeffersonian view of government that the less is the better: "The best education for democracy will be the one which trains, disciplines, and teaches the least." Because human nature is good, traditional restraints are unnecessary, public education needs to transmit nothing, and a revolutionary anti-institutionalism is implicit. "For the necessary faculties are inborn and they are more likely to be perverted by too much culture than to wither for the lack of it." Because Lippmann argued that the democratic utopianism of modern revolutionaries could never be fulfilled in the real world, it seemed to him inevitable that sooner or later someone would reach the conclusion of the Bolsheviks "that utopia must be brought about by an indefinitely prolonged process of unlimited revolution which would exterminate all opposition, actual and potential." This is what Lippmann meant by saying that the "totalitarian tendency has always been present and logically implied in the modern revolutionary movement."

Essays in the Public Philosophy was Lippmann's heaviest assault on relativism and his most forthright absolutistic espousal. No less than in the 1930s did he argue the practical necessity of adhering to liberal democratic traditions which were endangered. Indeed Lippmann defended belief in his moral absolutes during the 1950s largely on pragmatic grounds. But he also rooted the ethics of what he called the traditional Western public philosophy in natural law. On the one hand, liberal society could not work without belief in certain universal truths. On the other hand, these truths were not simply made up but rather exist in the nature of things. They can be ignored, but they cannot be eliminated. Insofar as there was a fusion of Lippmann's pragmatic and ideal justifications for belief in a universal ethical order, it occurred in his insistence that there *must* be moral truths because the Western tradition at its best said so. The principles of Lippmann's public philosophy, he said, "are the principles of right behavior in the good society, governed by the Western traditions of civility." Insofar as he spelled out the guidelines of the public philosophy, it was to indicate the public obligations, as well as the private rights, of the holder of property, and the duty not to lie and to willingly confront debate on the part of anyone exercising the right of free speech. In the case of the principles of private property as well as those of free speech, according to Lippmann, a rational order was assumed in which sincere inquiry could ascertain universally good public policy. He admitted that it was "possible to organize a state and conduct a government on quite different principles," but he claimed that "the outcome will not be freedom and the good life."[18] Phrased too generally to offer precise advice on domestic American problems in the 1950s, *The Public Philosophy* served mainly as an argument that the West had to reaffirm its commitment to freedom, as traditionally understood, in opposition to totalitarianism. Readers were left to guess for themselves just exactly how conservative and how supernatural were the implications of Lippmann's public philosophy.

Given his philosophic perspective, including the significance of the idea of totalitarianism, it might be supposed that Lippmann would have become as much a Cold Warrior as William Henry Chamberlin and Sidney Hook. It is true that, toward the end of World War II, Lippmann did momentarily talk as if moral absolutes were going to dominate his attitude toward American foreign policy and that he might deny the possibility of cooperation with Russia. Earlier in the war, he had followed most commentators in emphasizing the lack of importance of differing national philosophies in the practical workings of international affairs. Looking back in 1943 at a long history of doctrinal contrasts between Tsarist autocrats and Bolshevik revolutionaries, on one side, and, on the other, American constitutional democrats, Lippmann stressed in *U.S. Foreign Policy: Shield of the Republic* that peace and even occasional cooperation had characterized the historical relations of the two countries. "The story of Russian-American relations is an impressive demonstration of how unimportant in the determination of policy is ideology, how compelling is

---

[18] Walter Lippmann, *Essays in the Public Philosophy* (Boston: Little, Brown, 1955), pp. 13, 14, 20, 23, 46, 69, 75, 81, 124.

national interest."[19] But, when during the following year he looked ahead to postwar relations, he raised the question of how "national interests" should be defined. In implicit deference to the idea of totalitarianism, he said that until the Communists allowed "elemental civil rights" in areas under their control, there could not be "true collaboration" between the United States and the Soviet Union. Instead, there could be "only a *modus vivendi*, only compromise, bargains, specific agreements, only a diplomacy of checks and counter-checks," he wrote in *U.S. War Aims* in 1944. From a narrow perspective of national security, it might have been argued that such a *modus vivendi* should have been sufficient, but obviously Lippmann was for the moment not unequivocally adopting the narrow pragmatic perspective. His idea was that totalitarianism was an immoral absolute which he hoped would be everywhere rejected and which he declared had to be rejected if the "distrust which is ancient and deep" between "Russia and the Western world" were to be dispelled. "By one means alone can the distrust be in the end dissolved, and that is by the acceptance and avowal of the same ultimate standards of value," wrote Lippmann. "Only the inviolability of the human spirit can ever be the criterion of a universal standard."[20] Here, as the war was still raging (the book was written before the Allied invasion of France), was the ideology and rhetoric of the Cold War. It is true that in 1944 Lippmann was more hopeful than he had been previously, or was to be later, that the Soviets would in fact move away from their totalitarianism and embrace his postulated universal liberal values, which he felt they had already vowed to do. But it is more important to realize that Lippmann's prospectus for the postwar years assumed the necessity of worldwide recognition of his moral absolutes.

When the Cold War actually developed, on the other hand, Lippmann's explicit focus was strategic rather than ethical, and it was from this perspective that he criticized American policy. As soon as George Kennan's famous *Foreign Affairs* article, "The Sources of Soviet Conduct," outlining the official American policy of "containment," was published in 1947, Lippmann attacked it on the grounds that Kennan was "exclusively preoccupied with the Marxian ideology, and with the communist revolution." Lippmann argued that Kennan's policy was based upon the assumption that there had to be continual war with the Soviet Union until there ceased to be ideological differences between Russia and the West. "The history of diplomacy is the history of relations among rival

---

[19] Walter Lippmann, *U.S. Foreign Policy: Shield of the Republic* (Boston: Little, Brown, 1943), pp. 138–139.

[20] Walter Lippmann, *U.S. War Aims* (Boston: Little, Brown, 1944), pp. 140, 141, 152.

powers, which did not enjoy political intimacy, and did not respond to appeals to common purposes," said Lippmann in criticism of Kennan's alleged assumption.[21] There was no denial on Lippmann's part in 1947 of the idea of Communist totalitarianism, but in contrast to his own position in 1944 and in criticism of Kennan's in 1947, he denied its relevance as the foundation of American foreign policy. It was the ending by negotiation of the presence of the Red army in eastern Europe, rather than the existence of Soviet totalitarianism or Communist ideology, which according to Lippmann in 1947 was the proper focus of American foreign policy. As the Cold War progressed into the 1950s, Lippmann continued to criticize the historic American propensity for turning foreign policy into a crusade, for magnifying particular diplomatic disputes into universal battles of righteousness versus evil, or what he called "the Wilsonian ideology." He explained in 1952 that the "Wilsonian system of ideas does not recognize that America is one nation among many other nations with whom it must deal as rivals, as allies, as partners."[22] Again at the end of the 1950s Lippmann addressed himself to "the fallacy of assuming that this is one world and that the social order to which one belongs must either perish or become the universal order of mankind."[23] In other words, Lippmann's idea of totalitarianism as the embodiment of absolute evil, which was much like William Henry Chamberlin's, did not lead Lippmann after 1945 to view America's foreign policy toward the Soviet Union any differently from what his view would have been in Russia had not been considered totalitarian. Thus, as the contrast between Lippmann and Chamberlin clearly shows, the same idea of totalitarianism held by two people did not determine that they would espouse the same foreign policy.

STABILITY, RETROGRESSION, AND THE PROBLEM OF VALUES: RICHARD HOFSTADTER

Interpretations of history reflect in significant respects the climate of opinion in which the histories are written. Historian James Harvey Robinson, discussed in Chapter 2, proposed during the early 1900s a kind of reform-oriented scholarship which was consistent with his optimistic hopes for mankind. He announced that the forces of light in the world were the agents of change, and that the forces of darkness were the

---

[21] Walter Lippmann, *The Cold War: A Study in U.S. Foreign Policy* (New York: Harper, 1947), pp. 31, 60.

[22] Walter Lippmann, *Isolation and Alliances: An American Speaks to the British* (Boston: Little, Brown, 1952), pp. 21–27, 22.

[23] Walter Lippmann, *The Communist World and Ours* (Boston: Little, Brown, 1959), pp. 50–51.

conservative agents of the existing order. He asked that historians expose those contemporary beliefs and institutions which may have been relevant to conditions in the past, but which were no longer relevant to the present. Written histories could then become a usable past for today's reformers.

Because most American intellectuals absorbed the progressive climate of opinion during the early decades of this century, scholars produced dozens of books and articles that preached Robinson's message. Most dramatically, Charles Beard provided *An Economic Interpretation of the Constitution of the United States* (1943), in which he explained how the Constitution was written by men who wished to protect their vested economic, political, and social interests at a particular point in time. Readers were left to make the inference that however relevant the Constitution was to those men in 1787, it was no longer relevant to the increasingly democratic American society in an urban and industrial twentieth century. During the years of protest in the early 1900s when the courts were striking down reformers' legislation on the grounds that it violated the Constitution, Beard's scholarly history amounted to an exposé. More broadly, Beard himself and other scholars extended Robinson's progressive view to the entire sweep of American history. The stark conflict between bad conservatives, who appealed to selfish interests, and good reformers, who appealed to the general welfare, became the characteristic explanation for historical change. And change, when it was not a conservative counterattack, was assumed by most progressives to be betterment.

But the emergence of the idea of totalitarianism during and after the 1930s had severe implications for the optimistic assumptions on which the progressive interpretation was based. The European revolutionary dictatorships were clearly agents of change. Communist sympathizers insisted that dictatorships of the Left were forward-looking whereas dictatorships of the Right were reactionary, which allowed those on the Left to retain the basic progressive view. But as most American intellectuals became increasingly convinced that in practice the brutality of the Communists was equivalent to the inhumanity of the Fascists, change lost its moral claim. The ethical question became not whether there was change, but how one evaluated it. Change as a result of revolution appeared to lead to dictatorship; dictatorship seemed unwilling to yield its power; its power was perceived as destructive of valued individual rights. Whether the dictatorial power was justified in the name of the proletariat or the master race came to seem inconsequential. Further undermining the assumptions of the old progressive interpretation was the apparent fact that the revolutionary dictatorships had the support of their subjects. Faith in the judgment of the people had been part of the progressive optimism. If change in much of the modern world was likely retrogressive rather than progressive, and if masses of men seemed not to know the difference, on what could the moral man rely? What did this mean for a historian's interpretation of the American past?

Richard Hofstadter (1916–1970), perhaps the most widely read American historian in the fifties and sixties, was sympathetic to the progressive view of the past when he was a young scholar in the late 1930s and 1940s. His first historical researches explored the relationship between ideas and the environments which produced them, and he expressed Beard's delight in uncovering selfish political and economic interests behind statements of official policy and public philosophy. Coupled with Beard's influence in Hofstadter's background was a socialist perspective. In a preface to a book on *The American Political Tradition* in 1948, which was composed of sophisticated essays debunking in a Beardian fashion various political leaders, Hofstadter argued that mainstream American politics had always operated within the confines of a capitalistic system. "However much at odds on specific issues, the major political traditions have shared a belief in the rights of property, the philosophy of economic individualism, the value of competition," he wrote; "they have accepted the economic virtues of capitalist culture as necessary qualities of man."[24] This statement, which minimized the significance of political conflict in American history, was not characteristic of progressive scholarship, and in fact represented a serious logical and theoretical challenge to it. But it is symptomatic of the ambiguous relation between American reform thought and socialism that neither Hofstadter nor anyone else at the time dwelled on the contradiction. Pieces of the socialist dream, and aspects of the socialist critique, had always been picked up by progressive reformers without much thought for their logical and theoretical implications. If the whole society shared the same capitalistic values, and if the rival political parties offered no significant alternatives, the progressive historians' preoccupation with conflicting groups had been misplaced. The Jeffersonian and Hamiltonian traditions had been perpetuations of Tweedledum and Tweedledee. But progressive scholarship had been critical enough of capitalism, and of politics that narrowly served the interests of business, so that Hofstadter's generalization concerning the capitalist consensus seemed, in John Higham's words, "only a step to the left."[25] The important feature was antagonism toward the influence exercised by dominant economic interests over national policy, and Hofstadter's writings shared this feature with the histories of progressives.

Yet the conclusion that American history was experienced within a

---

[24] Richard Hofstadter, *The American Political Tradition* (New York: Knopf, 1948), p. viii.

[25] John Higham et al., *History* (Englewood Cliffs, N.J.: Prentice-Hall, 1965), p. 213.

fundamental consensus had tremendous implications for reinterpreting the past. Louis Hartz spelled out these implications in sweeping terms in *The Liberal Tradition in America* in 1955, while retaining some of the criticism of the limitations of American values and behavior. Hartz argued that Americans had never known the extreme and violent alternatives of feudalism and leveling revolution offered by European history. Rather, Americans were from the first property-conscious individualists, acting out their history within the narrow confines of middle-class liberalism. Not the conflict of the progressives but the consensus of Alexis de Tocqueville marked the political thought of the United States. Hartz praised the consensus insofar as it had successfully avoided modern European revolutionary dictatorships, but he criticized American inflexibility and lack of imagination. He warned Americans that the limits of their experience would prevent understanding of contemporary events in Asia and Africa. The tradition of the United States was not shared by peoples in the newly developing nations, their behavior and values would not correspond to American standards, expectations, and desires, and the United States could not, without failure and disillusionment, hope to lead the world by its own example.

The more common application in the 1950s of the consensus perspective, however, was linked to social thought more favorable to the existing American order. Most baldly, in *The Genius of American Politics*, Daniel Boorstin celebrated the consensus which was America. Precisely because the United States was such a splendid practical success, "a decent, free, and God-fearing society," Americans had been free from the kind of doctrinaire conflict which characterized the history of Europe.[26] In one of the most dramatic illustrations of the conservative social thought of the 1950s, Boorstin (who was himself a Left radical in his youth during the 1930s) expressed more satisfaction with America than had any distinguished historian since George Bancroft a century before.

In a much more complicated and self-aware way, Richard Hofstadter, too, applied the consensus interpretation in the 1950s to American history in a manner which undermined the forces of reform. He did not explicitly stress historical consensus the way Hartz and Boorstin did, but his influential writings on political thought implied the lack of meaningful ideological alternatives in America's past. What he explicitly suggested was that leading reform movements viewed by progressive scholars as carriers of light and truth were significantly flawed. "I find that I have been critical of the Populist-Progressive tradition—more so than I would have been had I been writing such a study fifteen years ago," Hofstadter

---

[26] Daniel Boorstin, *The Genius of American Politics* (Chicago: University of Chicago Press, 1953), p. 4.

said in *The Age of Reform* in 1955. He expressed sympathy with the postwar intellectual temper of "liberals" who are "far more conscious of those things they would like to preserve than they are of those things they would like to change."[27] Hofstadter considered himself a friendly critic of reformers, analyzing from within, and he addressed himself to "liberals" who were likewise friendly. The fact is important for gauging the pervasiveness of the conservative climate of opinion in the 1950s. Hofstadter did not mean to reflect, any more than he meant to address his analysis to, the perspective of historic enemies of American reform—those whom he would label traditional "conservatives." The point is that the postwar temper, which severely qualified and undercut progressive reform, permeated the liberal intellectual community that had previously written and supported progressive thought.

Hofstadter devoted lengthy discussion to both the agrarian Populist and the urban Progressive movements in *The Age of Reform*. In both cases he brought forward provocative fresh interpretations which tarnished the idealized image of the reformers. The Populists had been customarily regarded as links between Jeffersonian Republicanism and Jacksonian Democracy, on one side, and the Progressive and New Deal movements on the other side, progenitors of humane, modern American reform. Hofstadter admitted the social achievements of the Populists, as well as those of the Progressives, but he emphasized what he regarded as defects of the Populist mentality. The Populists were narrow, suspicious, unsophisticated provincials, he suggested. All too willing to believe that conspiracies among capitalists and businessmen were responsible for cheating the farmers out of their rightful profits, the Populists were also guilty of a naive and potentially dangerous faith in the ability of direct popular action to right society's wrongs. Further, Populist rhetoric betrayed a latent anti-Semitism traceable not so much to malice or familiarity with Jews but more to the characteristic distrust of outsiders felt by the hinterland. Hofstadter's Populists were viewed, as eastern urban thought in the late nineteenth century tended to regard the western farmers, no longer as the "backbone" but as the "boneheads" of the nation. Hofstadter undermined the claims of the Progressive reformers differently. He pioneered in the sociological and psychological interpretation of political history by arguing that outstanding Progressives were suffering from a loss of status and power due to basic social changes. In an attempt to regain prestige and influence, these Progressives unconsciously were attracted to a reform movement which they could lead and in which, at the same time, they could criticize some of the aspects of the new order that they did not like. Not positive reform ideals but rather unconscious social

---

[27] Richard Hofstadter, *The Age of Reform* (New York: Knopf, 1955), pp. 12, 14.

position and psychological response were thus more important, Hofstadter suggested, in understanding the reformers.

What was the relevance of these subtle and imaginative reinterpretations of reformers to the social thought of the 1950s? By his own testimony, Hofstadter meant simply to enrich historical understanding and to sharpen the sensitivity of reformers themselves. But it was possible to draw inferences of a most conservative nature from *The Age of Reform*, and, given the postwar climate of opinion, such conservative inferences were freely drawn. Hofstadter tended to depict reformers as living in some form of maladjustment to their society. He did not pretend to give a complete history of all facets of the protest movements. Nonetheless the emphasis on maladjustment implied that the problem was the reformers' rather than society's. To the extent that the Populists were economically disadvantaged by agricultural overproduction, for instance, their attack on middlemen, railroads, banks, eastern businessmen, and Congress was at best gratuitous. The implication was that farmers, not society, were malfunctioning. To the extent that Progressives were nostalgically protesting their own loss of status in a new urban, industrial order, the objective social conditions were irrelevant. The spotlight, once again, was on the maladjustment of the reformer.

What explains, apart from the internal history of the scholarship itself and his attempt to deepen historical understanding, Hofstadter's emphases and the inferences made by readers in the 1950s? The impact of the idea of European totalitarianism upon Hofstadter, as well as upon Louis Hartz and Daniel Boorstin, was great. The history of the United States appeared most different, and most commendable, insofar as it was free from European dictatorships of the Left and Right. American society thereby gained a moral claim which earlier progressive historians had never given it. It was, by definition, mainstream American traditions which were responsible for this country's escaping the blight of totalitarianism. Protests against the status quo had to this extent to justify their criticisms. The progressives' assumption that moral superiority rested with protesting reformers was undermined and indeed reversed. Further, in the case of Hofstadter's portrait of Populism, elements of the reform mind were seen as at least remotely similar to what was feared in European totalitarianism. Conspiracy theories, anti-Semitism, and demands for direct action were viewed against the background of European revolutionary dictatorships.

In addition, Hofstadter and many others in the intellectual community discovered contemporary manifestations of what they thought was a native American tendency toward totalitarianism during the late 1940s and early 1950s. What seemed to William Henry Chamberlin and Sidney Hook to be an understandable and frequently proper investigation of individual loyalty and national security appeared to many intellectuals to be, particularly in the exaggerated form taken by McCarthyism, a dangerous attempt to impose totalitarian thought control upon Americans. Thus the conservative impulse, defined as the attempt to keep the traditional American democratic system free from new threatening totalitarian characteristics, was revealed in Hofstadter's writings during the 1950s.

5

A NEW RADICALISM,
A NEW BOHEMIANISM, AND
A NEW IDEA OF TOTALITARIANISM
IN THE 1960s

As the Great Depression in the 1930s quickly made the decade of the 1920s seem strangely remote, so the crises of the 1960s and 1970s have made the decade and a half following World War II appear equally distant. Especially to those younger Americans who are currently most critical of the existing order, the late forties and fifties seem a period of almost unrelieved crassness, stupidity, and immorality, exactly as young social critics during the 1930s saw little in the twenties to redeem that decade in their eyes.

The period after World War II was of course more complex than the unsympathetic stereotype given by today's radicals. But, as the preceding chapter argued through its biographical sketches, the social thought of the postwar years was conservative in various significant respects. This generalization is not weakened by the fact that most of the leading social thinkers called themselves "liberals" of one kind or another, and that they frequently opposed others whom they called "conservatives." Not only in relation to their own previous radical or reformist social thought, but also strictly on the basis of the ideas in their postwar writings, such intellectuals as William Henry Chamberlin, Sidney

Hook, Walter Lippmann, and Richard Hofstadter contributed to the dominant conservative mood of the late 1940s and 1950s.

Protest against American involvement in Vietnam, racial discrimination at home, poverty in an affluent society, pollution of the natural environment, traditional patterns of education, and customary personal styles of life marked the emergence in the 1960s of a new radicalism in social thought. Often labeled a new revolt of the young, it is both less and more than that. Only a minority of the young people under thirty have participated in or expressed sympathy for political dissent and the search for a new life-style. "The young radicals and hippies" have been in fact a small proportion of their age-group, mainly college students, dropouts, and hangers-on around universities. But, like traditional intellectuals in relation to the whole society from which they have frequently been estranged, the young radicals have had an influence exceeding their numerical importance. This is because their social critique is not merely a function of generational conflict. The success of (and the overall society's preoccupation with) the young dissenters is explained in part by the extent of outright sympathy among some, ambivalence among more, and tolerance on the part of yet more, members of older generations of Americans—particularly in the academic world. To put it in historical terms, today's new radicalism and new bohemianism have their roots firmly in the soil of earlier twentieth-century social thought and thus go deeper than the apparent origins in a conflict of generations.

Both the bohemianism and the political radicalism of the contemporary American scene are almost as venerable as the more conservative elements of the existing order. The widespread search for a more innovative way to live, one less restricted by traditional financial, social, and sexual patterns, is now more than a half-century old in the United States. Many members of several generations of liberal arts college students, writers and artists in big city bohemias, and academicians and professional people have by this time variously rejected some or all of the Horatio Alger myth and the personal dictates of Victorian respectability. The number of the young and middle-aged who show the external signs of the inward revolt is larger in the 1970s than ever before; the nature of the revolt against the dominant middle-class style of life remains the same. Today's articulate rebels phrase their denunciation of the work ethic, of the attempt to measure the success of a person's life by his material gains, of the inequality of women and the stultification inherent in conventional family and sexual patterns, in the same terms as did the Greenwich Village bohemians in the days before World War I and through the 1920s.

The contemporary political radicalism traces its twentieth-century American source to the progressive and experimentalist temper of intellectuals associated with the reform movement prior to World War I, although today's radicals are critical of attempts merely to reform rather than to reconstruct radically the economic, political, and social system. In this sense the Communists and other extremists of the 1930s provide the closest parallels to the radicals of the sixties and seventies. The major distinction is that the Old Left perpetuated little of the bohemianism which characterized the estranged intellectuals of the 1920s, whereas many of today's radicals have assimilated the search for new personal styles of life.

FROM THE OLD LEFT TO THE NEW: C. WRIGHT MILLS

Perhaps the best-known dissenter from the reigning conservatism of the 1950s was sociologist C. Wright Mills (1916–1962). Born and raised in Texas, and educated at the Universities of Texas and Wisconsin, he spent his short career after World War II at Columbia University. It was not as an academic sociologist that Mills became famous to a large audience of readers and a sort of intellectual godfather to a younger generation of radicals, however, but as a prolific social critic of all aspects of American life and public policy. His widely read books and essays sketched much of the outline which would be filled in by the New Left after Mills's death. Because of his social views, Mills was customarily viewed as an anachronism in the 1950s. And indeed there was much of the old progressive muckraker in Mills, who delighted in exposing and lampooning the behavior of the rich and powerful, and there was a good deal of unreconstructed Depression radicalism in him too. But in retrospect it can be seen that Mills was a prophetic figure, unerringly attacking the aspects of contemporary thought that radicals of the 1960s and 1970s would later find most vulnerable: the idea of European totalitarianism, which by contrast celebrated American society as free and humane; American foreign policy in the Cold War; and the existing conceptions of scholarship and the role of the universities.

It was logically necessary for any considerable success of the New Left in the 1960s, speaking of the matter in terms of an intellectual debate, that the idea of European totalitarianism which emerged from the 1930s and which became popular in the postwar years had to be undermined. No radical ideology could make headway as long as any proposal for drastic change was saddled with the onus of totalitarianism and while America was defined in terms of its opposition to totalitarianism. What obviously was needed was the development of a viewpoint which minimized the significance of the difference between "them" and "us," which specifically eroded the contrast between Soviet totalitarianism and American democracy. Mills provided the framework for such a viewpoint in the 1950s, although he frequently stated that American society was not yet as closed a system as Fascist and Communist totalitarian societies. At the time the dominant intellectual temper rejected his perspective, but by the late 1960s the radicals had assimilated it into a rhetoric which easily and contemptuously spoke of American totalitarianism. "We" had become "they" in the eyes of the New Left, and the transformation of an old idea of totalitarianism into a new one was symptomatic of a new climate of radicalism.

What C. Wright Mills said in effect was that the older idea of European totalitarianism, and the accompanying affirmation of constitutional democracy in the United States, were more the expression of shallow piety than of realistic analysis. The form, he argued, rather than the actual functioning, of American life was unduly spotlighted. In fact, almost all Americans failed to exercise the public freedoms to which in theory they were entitled, and real power over public policy was held by few. Mass society, characterized by the population's passivity, the lack of individual opinions, and the inability to respond or object to manipulation on the part of the authorities, was found at its most extreme in Nazi Germany or the Soviet Union. In the United States the characteristics of the mass society were increasing, according to Mills, with the result that the idea of citizen participation in a democratic process simply no longer fit the facts. Almost no information was available to the citizenry except that provided by the mass media, and independent judgment became increasingly rare. Individuals thought in terms of stereotypes which were supplied by the opinion makers. The thoughtlessness of the individual was related to the loss of independence, which was psychological as well as intellectual. The typical mass man in the United States, and elsewhere, Mills wrote in *The Power Elite* (1956), "loses his independence, and more importantly, he loses the desire to be independent: in fact, he does not have hold of the idea of being an independent individual with his own mind and his own worked-out way of life." Because the individual does not create his own life, his daily existence seems to him more or less meaningless. Indeed he becomes increasingly lost, according to Mills, because "life in a society of masses implants insecurity and furthers impotence; it makes men uneasy and vaguely anxious."

There was a curious similarity between Mills's pessimism concerning the state of contemporary democracy and Walter Lippmann's jeremiad on the common man in *Essays in the Public Philosophy*. Both agreed that democracy had not worked successfully because of the lack of intelligent and effective participation of the citizenry. But whereas Lippmann blamed the failure on men themselves, Mills attributed it to the manipulation of men by those who held power in society. Lippmann said America needed a power elite; Mills said that unfortunately the United States already had one.

The masses of Americans, according to Mills, made no effective use of their theoretical democratic rights to govern themselves, and thus the conservative defense of the American political system in terms of representative democracy was a defense of form rather than function. Actual power in the United States had fallen into the hands of a relatively small group of men by the twentieth century. "Official commentators like to contrast the ascendancy in totalitarian countries of a tightly organized clique with the American system of power," Mills wrote in *The Power Elite*. "Such comments, however, are easier to sustain if one compares mid-twentieth-century Russia with mid-nineteenth-century America," he continued. The contemporary American power elite was composed of an interlocking directorate of corporate, military, and political leaders. All important decisions of national policy were made by these men, who occupied the most responsible positions in their various institutions. Because of the complex nature of contemporary society the institutions were dependent upon one another, and their leaders were thus members of a common group of decision makers. A foreign policy judgment by politicians was equally an economic judgment by business leaders and a military judgment by generals and admirals, and it therefore brought the elites together. Sociologically, members of the power elite were relatively homogeneous:

> They derive in substantial proportions from the upper classes, both new and old, of local society and the metropolitan 400. The bulk of the very rich, the corporate executives, the political outsiders, the high military, derive from, at most, the upper third of the income and occupational pyramids. Their fathers were at least of the professional and business strata, and very frequently higher than that. They are native-born Americans of native parents, primarily from urban areas, and, with the exceptions of the politicians among them, overwhelmingly from the East. They are mainly Protestants, especially Episcopalian or Presbyterian.[1]

The homogeneous elite led, and the masses followed. American democracy was an illusion, an illusion which contributed to the perpetuation of the rule of the power elite.

Mills was not specific in *The Power Elite* concerning why the nature of American leadership led to the particular policies that were adopted. He merely mentioned such decisions as Franklin Roosevelt's foreign policy prior to World War II and Harry Truman's decision to drop the

---

[1] C. Wright Mills, *The Power Elite* (New York: Oxford, 1956), pp. 323, 271, 279.

atomic bomb on Hiroshima. Nor did Mills explore in detail the process of decision making itself. Rather, he documented at length the fact that the power elite was not representative of the population at large in social, economic, religious, and ethnic characteristics. Mills's summary of social attributes might appear too vague to help understand why particular public policies would be pursued, and others rejected. But Mills implied that the common background of the power elite imposed the initial limitations upon the range of alternatives considered by the decision makers at any time. Whether the power elite made decisions which conflicted with the wishes of the masses of people, or accurately reflected the popular will, was not a question in Mills's argument because the masses were manipulated by those in power. American society was on the road to totalitarianism.

In Mills's attacks on the postwar foreign policy of the United States he came closest to tying the composition of the power elite to specific decisions, and he anticipated the criticisms of the radicals of the 1960s and 1970s. It was generally accepted that the American economy had recovered from the Great Depression only because of the stimulation of World War II, and Mills argued that prosperity had continued in the 1940s and 1950s largely because of continued defense spending. Fear of recession influenced corporate leaders to favor increased military expenditures. Further, for many businesses, such as aircraft, missile, and electronic corporations, few markets existed aside from the military. And defense spending had the extra advantage to all capitalists that it did not compete with private enterprise, in contrast to other stimulants to the economy such as government welfare spending. Thus, perpetual preparation for war guaranteed high profits for the corporate elite. But Mills argued that the business leadership was only part of the interlocking directorate. "I am *not* suggesting that military power is now only, or even mainly, an instrument of economic policy," he wrote in *The Causes of World War Three* in 1958. "To a considerable extent, militarism has become an end in itself and economic policy a means to it." The economic and military elite, most importantly, with the support of the political elite, were joined in constantly increasing preparation for war. "In the meantime, an expensive arms race, under cover of the military metaphysic and in a paranoid atmosphere of fright, is an economically attractive business," Mills wrote. The specific significance for public policy of a permanent war economy was that it would probably result in the very war which it was allegedly designed to avert. "The immediate cause of World War III is the military preparation of it," declared Mills.

He held the Soviet power elite at least as responsible as the American leadership for the Cold War and the coming of the next war, but his discussion of the Russians was essentially free of contemporary Cold War castigation of the Soviet Union as uniquely totalitarian. Indeed, at the same time as he depicted American movement down the totalitarian road, he suggested that the Soviets were advancing out of Stalin's dark night. There were echoes of the old radicals' progressive and pragmatic defense of the Bolshevik dictatorship in the 1920s and 1930s in Mills's emphases in the 1950s upon Russia's special problems, her recent dramatic economic growth, and the conviction of her people that conditions would improve in the future. Mills specifically suggested that the Soviet economy would before long bring "higher and more equalitarian standards of living," with the result that "greater political and cultural freedom" would follow: "first because of the greater social efficiencies which such freedom provides, and second because of the political pressures of the highly educated population that the Soviet Union is going to have."[2]

Reminiscent too of the earlier progressive and pragmatic defense of revolutionary dictatorship was Mills's book concerning Fidel Castro's Cuba, entitled *Listen, Yankee*, based upon a summer month of travel and conversations in Cuba in 1960. Mills's perspective was basically the same as that of a sympathetic American visiting the Soviet Union in the 1920s and 1930s. Feeling that the unsympathetic American press failed to report accurately what was going on, Mills wanted to discover and convey what the Cubans themselves thought about Castro's revolution. Not the "whole truth," nor an "objective appraisal," was Mills's purpose, but rather the Cuban revolutionary view of the matter. The "truth, whatever it turns out to be, is still being created, and every week it changes," he wrote in typical pragmatic fashion. "The true story of the Cuban revolution, in all its meaning, will have to wait until some Cuban, who has been part of it all, finds the universal voice of his revolution." As Lincoln Steffens and William Henry Chamberlin viewed the Soviet Union in the 1920s as an experiment which had to be seen from the standpoint of the experimenters, so Mills adopted a relativistic perspective toward Castro's revolution. Ostensibly reflecting a postponement of judgment until the experiment was completed, the view in both cases was rooted in fundamental sympathy for the avowed aims of the revolution.

Mills's interpretation of Cuba was presented in *Listen, Yankee* in the form of "letters" written by composite or typical revolutionaries to Americans. Historic American imperialism in the Caribbean, Batista's cruel dictatorship with the support of the United States, and Castro's heroic rebellion were recounted. Included in the "letters" were passages expressing Mills's personal admiration for the act of revolutionary will, passages

---

[2] C. Wright Mills, *The Causes of World War Three* (New York: Simon and Schuster, 1958). Quotations are from the revised edition (1960), pp. 67, 68, 90, 105.

which would later in the 1960s and 1970s exactly capture the sentiments of young American radicals:

> Since we [the mythical Cuban revolutionaries] did not belong to the old left intelligentsia—the older men who had gone through Communism and been disillusioned with Stalinism and with the purges and the trials and the 35 years of all that—we've had one enormous advantage as revolutionaries. We've not gone through all that terribly destructive process; we have not been wounded by it; and so we are free.[3]

Consistent with this escape from history, Mills's revolutionary letters defended Castro's postvictory execution of Batista supporters in precisely the same terms as the Old Left defended Bolshevik liquidations in the 1920s and 1930s. "Maybe in easy moral terms, *no* killing is excusable," the revolutionary letter said, but "the purposes and results of killing are quite different in different places and at different times." Besides, Americans have always killed others in their continual wars, and the Cuban revolution was a war. "Remember, too, Yankee, that morals are easy to come by sitting in your quiet suburbs away from it all, protected from it all." Finally, postrevolution executions were justified in terms of self-protection against counterrevolution.

Mills's interpretation of Cuban conditions in 1960 was progressive as well as pragmatic, which again followed the pattern of the Old Left's view of the Soviet Union in the twenties and thirties. In addition to seeing the revolutionary dictatorship as an experiment, the Old Left was convinced that it was an experiment moving mankind in the right direction. "Before the triumph of the revolution, Cuba was a land of grief and fear and frequent horror," Mills wrote in one of his revolutionary letters. "Under the revolutionary Government and with it the people of Cuba are enormously happy." The society was being completely reconstructed. A citizen militia was replacing Batista's army; land was being redistributed; the educational system was in the process of reform. "Is our Cuba today a revolutionary dictatorship?" asked one of Mills's letters.

> Yes, we suppose it is. But to understand what this means, in the case of Cuba at least, you must understand several things about this world and about Cuba. In the most literal sense imaginable, Cuba is a dictatorship of, by, and for the peasants and workers of Cuba. That phrase, "dictatorship of workers and peasants," was turned into a lie by Stalin and under Stalinism. Some of us know that. But

---

[3] C. Wright Mills, *Listen, Yankee* (New York: McGraw-Hill, 1960), pp. 8, 43.

none of us is going about our revolution in that way. So, to understand us, you must try to disabuse yourself of certain images and
ideas of "dictatorship."[4]

Mills was seriously concerned about the problem of the transition from
the hopefully temporary dictatorship to another permanent form of government, but he assumed that such a transition would be made, and that it
would ultimately be democratic in nature.

To recount the parallels between Mills's defense of the Cuban revolution and the Old Left's justification of the Bolshevik dictatorship is to
make a point of intellectual history, not to pass a judgment that Cuba
equals the Soviet Union and that Mills equals the Old Left. The historian
of social thought tries (among other things) to locate important mental
patterns, to observe their appearance, demise, and recurrence. C. Wright
Mills carried an older progressive and pragmatic pattern through the
1950s, when intellectuals generally rejected it, into the 1960s, when it
would be expressed again by new radicals. It is a different kind of question, not so narrowly historical as critical, not so much answered by
knowledge of the past as by one's ideological perspective and assessment
of the facts of life in the present, to ask whether a particular pattern of
thought is wise or foolish. An evaluation of the pragmatic and progressive
outlook, for example, is influenced not only by one's conclusion concerning its internal coherence, but also by one's general sense of the world,
human nature and man's relations with his fellowman, and, finally, by an
assessment of concrete situations in which the progressive and pragmatic
rationale is invoked. The defense of the Soviet Union in progressive and
pragmatic terms during the 1920s and 1930s is today generally assessed
unfavorably because the facts of Russian history are customarily interpreted in such a way as to contradict it. Whether the same defense of
Cuba, or any other revolutionary dictatorship, in the 1960s, or 1970s,
appears equally foolish depends upon a reading of the available evidence,
as well as upon a more abstract ideological position. Is the contribution of
the intellectual historian devoid of any implications beyond description
and explanation of the nature of thought in the past? Strictly speaking,
yes. More broadly, however, the intellectual historian suggests the powerful influence of men's mental sets upon the way they perceive reality.
Indeed, the statement is virtually circular from the intellectual historian's
standpoint, as men have no other way to know reality. By describing and
explaining the patterns of men's thoughts, the historian suggests why the
facts in the past have been perceived in the way they have been. But this

---

[4] Mills, *Listen, Yankee*, pp. 51, 116, 118–119.

does not mean that overall historical patterns of thought, whether or not judged profound in their outlook by historians, may not include individual perceptions which are remarkably correct or even predictions of uncanny accuracy. To cite one illustration of prophecy from *Listen, Yankee*, Mills wrote, in the fall of 1960 in one of the Cuban revolutionary letters to Americans concerning the threat of American support for anti-Castro counterrevolution—eight months prior to the April 1961 Bay of Pigs invasion,

> The most likely thing your Government is dreaming of is some kind of indirect military action, secretly supporting mercenaries and Batista henchmen; something like they did in Guatemala a while back. This intervention wouldn't come from U.S. soil, but maybe from somewhere in Central America.[5]

If, as some pragmatists said, the value of historical interpretation and of contemporary social analysis ought to be determined by its ability to foresee the future, Mills's view of American-Cuban relations was better than most.

Given his pessimistic analysis of mass society in the United States, the dominance of the power elite, and the drift of American foreign policy, why did Mills write so prolifically on social issues? Because he had in general an earlier twentieth-century progressive confidence in the potential ability of men to make their own history. More specifically, Mills hoped that American intellectuals—for whom his books were written—could be persuaded to change their minds in the 1950s and in turn to help influence a change in the public policy of the United States.

Mills's view of the role of intellectuals was central to his overall position. He defined intellectuals objectively in the way of most sociologists: "scientists and artists, ministers and scholars"; or put more generally, "those who are part of the great discourse of reason and inquiry, of sensibility and imagination that in the West began in Jerusalem and Athens and Rome, and that has been going on intermittently ever since." Mills admitted that, as a matter of historical fact, intellectuals sometimes justified authority and sometimes criticized it. But in postwar America, Mills thought the intellectuals ought to be critical of public policy. "Other men can mutter, with much justification, that they find nowhere to draw the line, to speak the emphatic 'No,'" Mills wrote. "But it is the political and the intellectual job of the intellectual to draw just that line, to say the 'No' loudly and clearly." Although Mills was preoccupied in his writings with politics and economics, he personally ignored conventional middle-

---

[5] Mills, *Listen, Yankee*, p. 68.

class life-style. Mills echoed the estranged literary intellectuals of the World War I era when he wrote that the fact that the intellectual "is alienated is another way of saying that he is capable of transcending drift, that he is capable of being a man on his own."

It was precisely the lack of alienation on the part of most intellectuals from the public policy of postwar America which angered Mills. He objected to the earlier idea of European totalitarianism as a unique phenomenon of revolutionary dictatorship, which accompanied the decline of American radicalism and the celebration of the existing order in the United States. He objected to the conservative pattern of thought after World War II which cast doubt on the possibility of the reconstruction of society by emphasizing the things that could go wrong instead of what could go right:

> Intellectuals accept without scrutiny official definitions of world reality. Some of the best of them allow themselves to be trapped by the politics of anti-Stalinism, which has been a main passageway from the political thirties to the intellectual default of our apolitical time. They live and work in a benumbing society without living and working in protest and in tension with its moral and cultural insensibilities. They use the liberal rhetoric to cover the conservative default.[6]

The postwar universities, the academic disciplines with their increasing professionalism, and the typical scholar who defaulted in his responsibilities as an intellectual, all came under heavy attack from Mills. The universities had become a research arm of the federal government waging a destructive Cold War, on the one hand, and centers for vocational and technical training, which merely made the existing social order more efficient, on the other. The academic profession was much like any other governmental or industrial organization: bureaucratic, specialized, serving its own narrow purposes, which is to say fitting into the basic social order. The highly specialized scholar served masters other than his own and his students' general education. Professionalization of the academic disciplines trapped the professor and his student within ever more tight methodologies and technologies. The old-fashioned teacher-professor, insofar as he still existed, refused to ask the hard questions concerning the relation of learning to life, or, if he did ask them, he answered them in a way which suggested to students that little could be done to change society. In brief, the universities, the academic disciplines, individual scholars,

---

[6] Mills, *The Causes of World War Three*, pp. 143, 144, 145.

and intellectuals generally were both positively and negatively contributing to the disastrous state of American and world affairs. Positively, they were Cold Warriors. "What is required of us, as intellectuals," Mills wrote, "is that *we* stop fighting the cold war of self-coordinated technicians and hired publicists, of self-appointed spokesmen, of pompous scientists who have given up the scientific ethos for the ethos of war technology."[7] Negatively, the universities, scholars, and intellectuals generally were guilty of passivity. It was not merely a matter of institutional indifference to social problems, but also an intellectual refusal to recognize that the contemporary human condition could be improved by altering man's environment. Mills objected to the postwar tendency to emphasize man's problems as ultimately insoluble, as traceable to the limitations of human nature itself. Man's chief threat to his fulfillment, Mills argued, "today lies in the unruly forces of contemporary society itself, with its alienating methods of production, its enveloping techniques of political domination, its international anarchy—in a word, its pervasive transformations of the very 'nature' of man and the conditions and aims of his life." Because he insisted that man's major problems were due to the social environment, Mills's plea for scholars in the social sciences was to conceive their work consciously and energetically in terms of historical and analytical understanding of social structures, in order that they might locate and solve problems "of direct relevance to urgent public issues and insistent human troubles."[8] This is what Mills meant by a proper application of "the sociological imagination," an application not out of intellectual curiosity alone but rather formed by contemporary problems.

C. Wright Mills died in 1962 before he could see the emergence of a widespread New Left in the United States. But by 1960 he did correctly perceive the beginnings of a new radicalism. "Is anything more certain than that in 1970," wrote Mills in 1960 to an audience of fellow radicals in Britain, "our situation will be quite different, and—the chances are high—decisively so?" The agents of the trend toward the emergence of a New Left he accurately saw to be the intellectuals, not the workers. Further, he prophetically put his finger on the utopianism of the new radicalism, which he supported on the grounds that it offered the most detached perspective from which to judge and redirect the contemporary world. And of all the intellectuals it was the "young intelligentsia" around the world to whom Mills looked as the prime agents of future change. "Isn't all this," he asked, "isn't it something of what we are trying to mean by

---

[7] Mills, *The Causes of World War Three*, p. 163.

[8] C. Wright Mills, *The Sociological Imagination* (New York: Oxford, 1959), pp. 13, 21.

the phrase, 'The New Left'? Let the old men ask sourly, 'Out of Apathy—
into what?' The Age of Complacency is ending. Let the old women com-
plain wisely about 'the end of ideology.' We are beginning to move
again."[9]

THE RADICAL POLITICS OF HISTORY: HOWARD ZINN

C. Wright Mills's plea for scholarship that would be useful in changing contemporary society was soon to be abundantly answered by a number
of young American historians. Generally born during the years of the
Great Depression, coming of age intellectually during the 1950s, these
radical historians published their first books and articles in the 1960s. Not
members of any one school of historical interpretation, nor in complete
agreement on their larger views of reality and human possibility, these
New Left scholars can nevertheless be discussed meaningfully as a group.
Like the progressive historians of the early 1900s, whom the young scholars so closely resemble in many respects, the neoprogressive historians of
the 1960s and 1970s have been united mainly in their opposition to what
they regard as the accepted conservative scholarship of their day, and in
their plea that it ought to be replaced by a reform-oriented or radically
inclined scholarship.

James Harvey Robinson, Charles Beard, Vernon Louis Parrington,
and other progressive historians thought that traditional scholarship usually failed to make a contribution to pressing current issues through a
failure to connect the past to the present. Further, they objected to those
historical interpretations which justified the economic, political, and social
status quo. Differing in their interpretations of specific historical events
and ideas, progressive scholars agreed that men could make their own
future by remaking the environment in which they lived. The intellectual
creation in written histories of a past which explained the origins of ideas
and institutions in the present, and which at the same time kept alive
reformist traditions from the past that could give nourishment to change
flowering in the present, comprised the progressive historian's contribution
to reform.

It seemed to most leading historians of the 1940s and 1950s that the
progressive scholars let their partisan involvement in the reform polemics
of their own day unduly influence their views of the past. As discussed in
the sketch of Richard Hofstadter in the previous chapter, postwar historical writings differed from those of progressives in part because of the

---

[9] *Power, Politics and People: The Collected Essays of C. Wright Mills*, Irving Louis
Horowitz, ed. (New York: Oxford, 1963), pp. 257, 259.

descriptive emphases by the former upon consensus rather than conflict, continuity rather than change, and in part because of a generally more appreciative assessment of the American past—an assessment which included more criticism of reformers and less criticism of the opponents of reform. Progressive historians were accused of dividing the past into a struggle between good and evil, in which those opposed to reform were cast into darkness. Whereas progressive historians appeared obviously on the side of reform, historians during the fifties often seemed to deprecate the desirability of reform by minimizing its value, as well as its significance as a factor in the American past.

The young New Left historians' reinterpretations during the 1960s focused upon a variety of topics. Diplomatic historians argued that American foreign policy was formulated in response to economic interests, rather than to the idealism on which decision makers tried to defend it. The origins and development of the Cold War were argued to be at least as much attributable to American policy as to that of the Soviets. The actual significance of successful domestic political reform was minimized, and the moral importance of unsuccessful and more radical protest was maximized. The early twentieth-century progressive reforms were said to be conservative and self-interested: in part they reflected the narrow limits of middle-class sympathies; in part they reflected the power of big business. Much the same was said of the New Deal by the New Left historians. Rather than leading an administration devoted to fundamental change, Franklin Roosevelt executed a successful salvage operation to save capitalism, established privilege, and the inequality of wealth. By contrast, unsuccessful Populism was argued to be profoundly radical in its vision of humane possibilities for American life—and so it was defeated, as socialism and all other radicalisms have unfortunately been defeated in American history.

These brief indications of the nature of some New Left interpretations in the 1960s are sufficient to suggest their disagreement with the historians of the 1950s. The young radicals started from the assumption that the existing social order in the United States was bad, as compared to what it could be, rather than good, as compared to revolutionary dictatorships in Europe. Like the earlier progressive historians, the New Left saw their scholarship as a springboard for change. The major difference between the young radicals and the old progressives was that the earlier confidence that change could and would occur within the normal process of the system was weakened. Accompanying this reduced faith in the self-reforming ability of the existing order, on the part of the New Left, was a preoccupation with the outcasts, the dispossessed, those for whom the American dream was a cruel hoax. Though there had been some concern by the old progressives over ethnic minorities, the role of women, and the perpetual poverty in American history, the young radical scholars were correct in saying that their own writings expressed more concern than the writings of any previous historians.

These general characteristics can be seen in detail by looking at the writings of one radical historian who, though a decade or more senior to most New Left scholars, has become an important spokesman for many younger radicals. Howard Zinn (1922–   ) has become one of the most active academic radicals, fusing participation in the civil rights movement and the protest over American policy in Southeast Asia with a carefully articulated, if extreme, expression of radical scholarship.

Zinn penned a most severe attack on scholars, and on his fellow historians in particular, for their basic irrelevance to the world in which they live. "Thanks to a gullible public," he wrote, "we have been honored, flattered, even paid, for producing the largest number of inconsequential studies in the history of civilization: tens of thousands of articles, books, monographs; millions of term papers; enough lectures to deafen the gods." The people, through state legislatures and alumni, continued to support scholars because they foolishly assumed that traditional scholarship was worthwhile. "Like politicians, we have thrived on public innocence." The waste of academic energies might be harmless if the world were not troubled, if social problems did not need the attention of scholars. But the contemporary social crisis demanded that all available intellectual resources be used, and meant that the conventional idea of scholarly detachment within an "ivory tower" university was morally indefensible.

Zinn criticized the concepts of "disinterested scholarship," "objectivity," "disciplinary specialization," "neutrality," and "rationality as opposed to emotionalism in scholarship." What these traditional ideals did was to remove the scholar from contemporary problems that would force him to realize his moral commitments and to try to implement them in his work. Thus scholarship on the sources of poverty would be interested, committed, interdisciplinary, and would reveal an emotional dimension both to the moral commitment and also to the understanding of the facts of poverty. "For a long time, the historian has been embarrassed by his own humanity," wrote Zinn. "Touched by the sight of poverty, horrified by war, revolted by racism, indignant at the strangling of dissent, he has nevertheless tried his best to keep his tie straight, his voice unruffled, and his emotions to himself." If the traditional ideals of detachment could be replaced by new ones of moral commitment, then the historian's schizophrenia could give way to socially useful scholarship.

The theoretical argument offered by Zinn in support of his plea for histories which would try to be of help in solving present problems traced its roots to the writings of early twentieth-century progressive scholars. But Zinn was perhaps even more contemptuous of traditional history than they had been, and he presented a more radical prospectus for his ideal future histories. He advocated a problem orientation for scholars, not unprecedented among historians, but Zinn explicitly stipulated that present-day problems should direct research into the past. In answer to traditional historians who would say that such "presentism" distorted the past along lines of the present's limitations and biases, Zinn responded that the historian could not in any case recapture the whole of the past. The only real question therefore was which criteria the historian used for selecting material. The historian will select, he will interpret the material he has selected, the selection and interpretation will reflect his limitations and biases, and these will in some sense have a relationship to contemporary society—if only by expressing disinterest and thus contributing to a perpetuation of the status quo. "Therefore the real choice is not between shaping the world or not, but between doing it deliberately or unconsciously." The fact was that most historians lived within a middle-class and liberal world for which detached scholarship was a cover allowing professional advancement and acceptance of the society's existing social and economic arrangements. "The scholar does vaguely aim to serve some social purpose, but there is an undiscussed conflict between problem-solving and safety for a man earning fifteen thousand dollars a year," according to Zinn. "There is no deliberate avoidance of social issues, but some quiet gyroscopic mechanism of survival operates to steer the scholar toward research within the academic consensus."

The definition, and examples, of present problems offered by Zinn for guidance in writing histories relevant to the contemporary world made clear how closely attuned to current affairs Zinn's ideal scholarship would be. He singled out the need for historians to select problems which would "intensify, expand, sharpen our perception of how bad things are, for the victims of the world." Historical research into the sufferings of the blacks and the poor would contribute to awakening people's sensibilities in the present:

> I see two values in going back. One is that dealing with the past, our guard is down, because we start off thinking it over and we have nothing to fear by taking it all in. We turn out to be wrong, because its immediacy strikes us, affects us before we know it; when we have recognized this, it is too late—we have been moved. Another reason is that time adds depth and intensity to a problem which otherwise might seem a passing one, susceptible to being brushed away. . . . If nothing else, it would make us understand in that black mood of

today what we might otherwise see as impatience, and what history
tells us is overlong endurance.[10]

Zinn candidly admitted that he was urging historians to select facts which
would, by themselves, tend to demonstrate suffering, discrimination, inequality, and injustice. He did not deny that facts existed which, by themselves, would tend to demonstrate the reverse. But he argued that historians should commit themselves to a better world, do their research in
an attempt to implement their view of a better world, and that they should
eschew "neutrality" or "objectivity" or "truth." "There are victims, there
are executioners, and there are bystanders," wrote Zinn. "In the
dynamism of our time, when heads roll into the basket every hour, what is
'true' varies according to what happens to your own head—and the 'objectivity' of the bystander calls for inaction while other heads fall." Thus,
unless "we wrench free from being what we like to call 'objective,' we are
closer psychologically, whether we like to admit it or not, to the execu-
tioner than to the victim."

Just as he thought it necessary for the historian to select evidence
concerning the dispossessed which corroborated the reformer's critique, so
Zinn singled out the need to "expose the pretensions of governments to
either neutrality or beneficence," because the public must be disabused "of
the confidence that they can depend on government to rectify what is
wrong." To accompany such a catalogue of governmental wrongdoing,
historical research should also chronicle "those few moments in the past
which show the possibility of a better way of life than that which has
dominated the earth thus far." Finally, Zinn's guidelines for radical histories included a search to "show how good social movements can go
wrong, how leaders can betray their followers, how rebels can become
bureaucrats, how ideals can become frozen and reified."

Zinn was fully aware of the relativistic implications of his statements
on historical scholarship. By denying that written histories derived enduring validity as a result of their relation to the evidence left from the past,
Zinn defined their value solely in terms of the present. Insisting that it was
preferable to influence actively the present instead of passively reflecting
it, he urged historians consciously to ransack the past in order to help
solve contemporary problems. With the best intentions, Zinn asked that
historians write propaganda for good causes. Zinn was apparently not
worried by the uses to which others might put actively presentistic histories. Just as Robinson and other progressive historians were saved from
a debilitating relativism by their faith in man's upward evolutionary

---

[10] Howard Zinn, *The Politics of History.* (Boston: Beacon, 1970), pp. 5, 15, 30–31,
32, 36, 38–39.

movement, which equated change and betterment, so Zinn seemed to assume that men could agree on the good things worth praising and the bad things worth excoriating. Or, to put it more exactly, since he knew very well that men did not agree on a definition of the good, Zinn's assertion of an ultimate moral absolutism accompanied his statement of written histories as merely instrumental. "To be truly radical is to maintain a set of transcendental beliefs (yes, absolutes) by which to judge and thus to transform any particular social system," he wrote.[11] Therefore, in much the same sense as was true of early progressive scholars, Zinn's view of the relativity of written history may have created theoretical problems for one looking at it from the outside; for believers on the inside, the new radical scholarship could be relative to the proper moral commitment and hence contributory to absolute truth.

Zinn's own writing has increasingly followed his directives for a radical history. His first book, originally a doctoral dissertation at Columbia University, was a conventional study of Fiorello LaGuardia in Congress during the 1920s. In 1956 he moved to Atlanta, Georgia, where he taught history at Spelman College, one of the black colleges at the Atlanta University Center. He became deeply involved in the civil rights movement, and out of this involvement during the late fifties and early sixties he wrote *The Southern Mystique,* an attack on the idea that the South, both black and white, is too complex and mysterious to attempt to reform. Zinn was pragmatically scornful of scholarly efforts to search for the cause of white Southern resistance to desegregation. "I will not tangle with *cause,* because once you acknowledge *cause* as the core of a problem, you have built something into it that not only baffles people, but, worse, immobilizes them." In other words, too much historical understanding of how things were in the past, and how they came to be, just diverts people's attention from problem solving in the present. Speaking much the way an early philosophical pragmatist would have done, or the way Sidney Hook did in the 1930s, Zinn said:

> Why not ignore cause as a general philosophical problem and concentrate on *result?* The point is devilishly, irreverently simple: if you can get a desired result, the mystery is gone. Stop fumbling with the *cause* of prejudice except for those aspects on which we can operate.[12]

In addition to being philosophically pragmatic, Zinn expressed a good deal of the old progressive confidence in man's potential mastery over

---

[11] Zinn, *The Politics of History,* pp. 40, 41, 42, 47, 51.
[12] Howard Zinn, *The Southern Mystique* (New York: Knopf, 1964), pp. 7, 13.

history and over his current situation. Writing of contemporary society's ability to free itself of white Southern racial patterns, he said that "we are powerful enough today, and free enough, to retain only as much of the past as we want." Zinn's optimism no doubt owed something to the brief successes of the civil rights movement in the early 1960s; but it owed something also to the more enduring progressive and pragmatic strain in modern American reform and radical thought.

The Southern Mystique, like Zinn's companion contribution to the civil rights movement, SNCC: *The New Abolitionists* (1964), did not merely relate the past to the present; it was contemporary history. Zinn's belief that scholars, as well as participants, should attempt to write histories of current affairs, found expression in these books which publicized and provoked support for contemporary social protest and change. Consistent with Zinn's presentism, but developing it into a futurism, his *Vietnam: The Logic of Withdrawal* (1967) tried to outline how the United States could extricate itself from Southeast Asia. Following an analysis of current American policy in Vietnam, Zinn's concluding chapter consisted of a speech for President Lyndon Johnson to give to the nation justifying his hypothetical decision to terminate the war by immediately withdrawing American troops.

A critic of Zinn's theory of scholarly activism, or action scholarship, might ask if Zinn really believed—as a scholar, rather than as an activist —that white Southern resistance to Negro equality was only an illusion which reformers could dissolve, or if the United States could actually withdraw from Vietnam without counterbalancing repercussions. Zinn had after all said, a critic might continue, that a moral and reform-minded scholar ought to select those facts which buttressed his position. Thus, were there also facts which tended to suggest that white Southern resistance to Negro equality was well-nigh insuperable, or that immediate American withdrawal from Southeast Asia was impossible? Zinn's answer to such questions would have to be that the scholar could not be separated from the activist, if he were to fulfill Zinn's ideal of the moral scholar. Therefore Zinn's own writings on the past and the present, if consistent with his theory of action scholarship, would have to be considered intentionally propagandistic.

LIFE-STYLE AND THE REVOLUTION: JAMES SIMON KUNEN

It is much easier to explain the thought of contemporary radicalism as it expresses itself on matters of politics or scholarship than it is to delineate the mood of what may be called the new bohemianism of the current scene. Yet to stress only the ideas of those radicals who are principally concerned with public affairs would be to miss one whole dimension of the assault being mounted against the existing order in the United States. Accompanying the new political radicalism of figures such as C. Wright Mills and Howard Zinn, and sometimes to be found in the political radicals themselves, has been a preoccupation with more or less basically changing one's personal style of life. In the extreme form of "hippie" withdrawal from conventional behavior patterns, the new bohemians have created a minor social movement, at least among the young. In its more moderate and most pervasive form, some middle-aged as well as many young Americans have subjected their personal values and mores to unprecedented examination. This has been done usually without "dropping out" and may or may not be accompanied by a sympathy for radical politics. From this search for a new life-style has come the most important nonpolitical attack upon the way Americans have traditionally lived.

It is almost impossible to place too much stress upon the importance of the Horatio Alger myth as the focus of attack by the current preoccupation with new life-styles. The significance of the Self-Help idea may be best explained by indicating the positive values it expresses, and the nature of reality which it assumes. According to the dictates of Self-Help, in its changing rhetorical dress from the Puritan doctrine of calling through Benjamin Franklin's aphorisms and Alger's novels to the rags-to-riches story of a Herbert Hoover or a Richard Nixon, the world was open and yet moral, to be economically exploited and yet limited by economic scarcity.

From the seventeenth century to the post-World War II era, the primary fact of life for most Americans was to be found in the struggle to overcome economic adversity. The material goods of life were assumed to be insufficient to go around. The Alger myth may be viewed in part as a strategy for coping with a world of economic scarcity. The myth stipulated that self-denial, self-sacrifice, hard work, discipline, protection against adversity by development of usable skills, punctuality, loyalty, courtesy, abstinence, and cleanliness would be rewarded in maturity or old age by economic security or affluence. It is fashionable, and indeed irresistible, to satirize an Andrew Carnegie's advice to get up early, work hard, refrain from idleness and drink, and thus to become a millionaire. It is however impossible to deny the relevance of the dictates of hard work and thrift in a situation of economic scarcity. Millions of Americans have gained, not a fortune, but a living for themselves and their families by the conventional and common sense precepts of Horatio Alger.

More than economic satisfactions, however, and more than merely a strategy for dealing with conditions of economic scarcity, were involved in pursuing the Alger formula. A moral world was assumed, as well as one of limited economic means. Whatever the case was in practice, the Self-Help myth emphasized in its preachment that the successful man was the good man. Earthly rewards were an external sign of inward grace. Consequently, an affluent man of middle or old age had the knowledge not merely that he had been the winner of a grubby struggle for survival, but that he was in every sense a better man than his less successful fellows. Again, the temptation to indulge in satire is inviting, but the Self-Help view was that the liar, the cheat, and the swindler would somehow be discovered and punished. Righteousness would be rewarded as if by Providence. It is the faith in this equation of the successful and the good which is at once so important to believers in the Alger myth and so egregious an example of hypocrisy in the eyes of critics.

The dignity accorded work by the Self-Help myth was perhaps its most important single idea. For the belief that a man is what a man does in his work, that his excellence can be measured by the achievement of his work, transcended situations of economic scarcity. Whatever its roots, the value of work has been traditionally cherished by Americans as a good in and of itself, as well as pragmatically useful to civilization, to one's mental health, and to economic success.

The critique of the Self-Help myth as a model of reality and as a moral guide is not new. But there have never been so many Americans, mainly younger but also older, who have rejected the values and the view of reality embodied in the Alger doctrine. For most white middle-class young people born during and after World War II, economic scarcity has not been a fact of life. There has not been a shortage of goods. Jobs, high salaries, educational scholarships for career training, and other signs of affluence have been generously available and have tended to undermine the imperative for the Alger tactics of self-denial, hard work, and thrift.

But the point is not merely that affluent younger Americans do not know a world of economic scarcity. By itself this would suggest simply that they lack economic preoccupations, or, to put it differently, that they take affluence for granted. In addition, a concern with what might be called psychological and spiritual scarcity has replaced preoccupation with economic scarcity on the part of those critical of the Alger myth. The life-style radicals insist that the myth has contributed to making American life psychologically and spiritually sterile, repressive, and impoverished.

The critique of the life-style radicals is that the Self-Help formula is part of an overly rationalized, inhumanly calculated social order. Children are brought up not to develop fully their emotional and esthetic potentialities, but to succeed as units of economic production and, increasingly, as technological specialists. The Alger formula for success, notwithstanding the relative absence of poverty for most young people of the white middle class, continues to be relevant for achievement in, say, engineering, medicine, and legal careers, indeed for most of the activities to which society accords respect. Moreover, the units of organization in which people work become ever larger, with the result that the already calculating Horatio Alger mentality is not much more than a computer part, a cog in a giant machine. Further, the older generations—which accept their roles as hard-working, clean, and punctual cogs in society's machines—are irrationally committed to the very system which dehumanizes them.

This strikes the new bohemians as paradoxical. The Alger myth, like all other expressions of the American dream, was meant to be a moral statement as well as a way of coping with the practicalities of the situation. White middle-class American parents have traditionally told their children that their American way of life was an attempt to realize high ideals as well as to achieve material abundance. More specifically, mainstream American culture has been moralistic in its rhetoric: altruism is superior to selfishness; inner satisfaction is preferable to external success; love is better than hate; people are worth more than anything else in the world. Yet it is precisely these moralistic shibboleths that the life-style radicals constantly invoke. The fact is that today's young life-style radicals are not only rebelling against the avowed values of their parents, as in the case of the Self-Help myth, but at the same time the young are taking, with what now appears to the parents to be dreadful and simplistic seriousness, the traditional moral rhetoric. From the perspective of the young, the more conservative older generations are guilty of hypocrisy insofar as they do not take their ideals seriously. Perhaps even more important, the older generations are now felt to be guilty of a betrayal. Originally the source of the ideals, they are now unsympathetic, even hostile and repressive, to the radicals who try to implement the ideals.

The obvious problem is that traditionally the precise means of implementing the ideals were not conceived in terms of today's life-style radicalism. It was customarily taken for granted that conventional mores would accompany attempts to fulfill avowed ideals. But there is a more elusive contrast present, too. It seems to many conservative Americans that the utopian psychological and spiritual preoccupations of the new bohemians reflect a misunderstanding of the nature of the world and of themselves, which at best renders their views superficial and at worst dangerous. At the very least, it is argued, the obsession with fulfillment of the spirit and the personality through personal relations, drugs, and innovative mores is foolishly romantic; at the most, the radicals are creating expectations and making demands on themselves and on others which are bound to result in failure and consequent disillusionment and despair. Optimistic when telling the radicals that life in America can be healthy and humane, the conservative reveals a deeper pessimism when he adds that the goal of psychological and spiritual rebirth is impossible to attain. The new bohemian, by contrast, offers a pessimistic analysis of contemporary America, but expresses a transcendent optimism about what could be achieved in the future.

These generalizations can to some extent be illustrated by an examination of one of the books from the younger generation of radicals, James Simon Kunen's *The Strawberry Statement: Notes of a College Revolutionary*, written in 1968, which was shortly thereafter made into a movie of the same name. Written in the form of a diary during the student uprising at Columbia University, *The Strawberry Statement* artistically documented the youthful concern with personal life-style, and demonstrated its relevance to political radicalism.

James Kunen (1948–   ) emerges from the pages of his diary as a Holden Caulfield of current radicalism. Adolescent Holden was the anti-hero of J. D. Salinger's *The Catcher in the Rye* in 1951, a tremendously popular novel in the fifties among young people. Characteristic of a long list of serious novels during the decade which portrayed the futile quest of an individual for personal identity and meaning in an indifferent world, *The Catcher in the Rye* was nonpolitical. But it is striking how similar an interpretation of the individual's lonely place in contemporary society was provided by the novelists of the conservative 1950s, as compared with the manifestly radical interpretation presented in the 1960s and   1970s. Holden Caulfield moved through prep school and New York City trying to live and to love, to discover and develop himself, offering the reader a perspective of irreducible humanity. Like Yossarian, Joseph Heller's anti-hero in *Catch-22*, published a decade after *The Catcher in the Rye*, Holden Caulfield could always spot the phony, the absurd, and the inhumane in society. The most significant contrast between the picture of reality offered by the best novelists of the fifties and the later radicals is that the former tended to accept the situation as part of man's inevitably tragic dilemma, whereas the latter have insisted that social conditions can and should be altered.

James Kunen said little in *The Strawberry Statement* of his background prior to the Columbia demonstration in 1968. "I wasn't always a radical leftist," he wrote. He had been a good student at Andover, a prep school in Massachusetts, rowed on the crew at Columbia, and if he participated in demonstrations against the draft, he also wrote letters for Eugene McCarthy's presidential bid in the spring before Columbia exploded. But even before he became radically involved, he was not particularly interested in his academic work at college. "I have just finished my Contemporary Civilization paper on 'The Abbot Benedict's *Regula* vs. Plato's Philosopher King,' " Kunen wrote as a freshman in 1966. "Five and a half hours producing a mammoth compost heap, a putrid dung-mound." As for life in New York City, he characterized its inhumanity and pointlessness with the image of a rat maze:

The city, where when you see someone on the subway you know you will never see him again. . . . The city, where you walk along on the hard floor of a giant maze with walls much taller than people and full of them. . . . It's a giant maze you have to fight through, like a rat, but unlike the rat you have no reward awaiting you at the end. . . .

And unlike the rat, you are not alone. You are instead lonely. There is loneliness as can exist only in the midst of numbers and numbers of people who don't know you, who don't care about you, who won't let you care about them.[13]

Against this personal background of Kunen's opposition to the Vietnam war, disinterest in academic routine, and criticism of the environment in which he lived, the disruption at Columbia occurred. Student demands that the university cease relations with the Institute for Defense Analysis, stop construction of a gymnasium to be built on the site of a public park between Columbia and Harlem, and that indoor protest demonstrations be allowed, were followed by noncompliance on the part of the administration, the occupation of buildings by students, occupation of the campus by New York police, and the confrontation of students and police.

The Strawberry Statement presents Kunen's involvement in, and reaction to, these events. He had nothing to do with the formulation of the initial student demands and he expressed no systematic political thought nor even a specific political position. His involvement as a militant protester was his response to the existence of the radical student demonstration, the refusal of the administration to comply, and the behavior of the police on campus. At each step his militancy, grounded originally in a vague dissatisfaction with his personal situation, life in America, and official university and government policy, increased until his identification with the radicals was most complete during battles with the police and his own arrests.

What explains this particular escalating response to events at Columbia, one so common and significant in all the violent confrontations on campuses around the country? The events themselves escalated, in severity, of course, as any participant would quickly answer. But that does not explain the direction in which Kunen's, or anyone else's, involvement moved. Not a developed political theory but a personal estrangement from the society established the direction of Kunen's movement. The hypocrisy of American ideals in the context of public policy at home and abroad, the absurdity of the Horatio Alger myth and the Victorian manners and morals with which it was associated, and the meaninglessness of the tradi-

---

[13] James Simon Kunen, *The Strawberry Statement* (New York: Random, 1969). Quotations are taken from Avon paperback (1970), pp. 27, 15, 11–12.

tional university, all predisposed Kunen to side with the protesters, critics, and victims, *if* a conflict erupted with the dominant order. Until radical leaders, the university administration, or the police precipitated a crisis, his alienation seemed to remain inactive.

Because Kunen's predisposition was personal and cultural rather than systematically political, his relation to the militant protesters was never a completely comfortable one. Throughout *The Strawberry Statement*, his concern for the individual human being recurred. He was sympathetic, curious, searching in his probing of motivation, questioning what he and his co-demonstrators were doing. During the student occupation of President Grayson Kirk's office, Kunen wrote:

> I do not know many people who are here, and I have doubts about why they are here. Worse, I have doubts about why I am here. . . . It's possible that I'm here to be cool or to meet people or to meet girls (as distinct from people) or to get out of crew or to be arrested. Of course the possibility exists that I am here to precipitate some change at the University.[14]

Later during the occupation of the President's office, he wrote a letter to his parents trying "to justify rebelling on my father's money." After arguing that it was his knowledge of history and philosophy that had led him to participate in the student protest, he realized "that my conception of the philosophy of law comes not so much from Rousseau as from Fess Parker as Davy Crockett":

> I remember his saying that you should decide what you think is right and then go ahead and do it. Walt Disney really bagged that one; the old fascist inadvertently created a whole generation of radicals.[15]

Kunen never altogether escaped the feeling that Hollywood had something to do with the Columbia revolution.

This is not to suggest that he lacked seriousness or depth of emotional involvement. It is to say that he was not a doctrinaire political radical, that he was as skeptical of much of the pretension of the protesters as of that of the older generation, that he was most energized at Columbia by specific things which happened to particular people, and that his more general political stance was of a most direct, uncomplicated moral sort. "There used to be a dream for America," he wrote. "People

---

[14] Kunen, *The Strawberry Statement*, p. 33.
[15] Kunen, *The Strawberry Statement*, p. 38.

should wake up and dream again." His view of American involvement in Vietnam reflected his approach to political problems.

> I don't understand why our government has us fight the war. . . . Are they incredibly evil men, or are they stupid, or are they insane? How can Johnson sleep? . . . Doesn't he realize that wars can't go well, that people always die in them and that's not well? Doesn't he know anything? . . . Wars are silly. They're ludicrous. . . . Why don't countries just stop it? Just cut it out, that's all. . . . All that's necessary is for the leaders to see what they've always done and are doing and for once know and feel and get sick and stop. Nobody fight any more. Of course it's not that simple. But I must be stupid because it seems that simple to me.[16]

The Vietnam war, in the same sense as the Columbia confrontation, served to fuse a primary concern for new life-styles to active political militancy on the part of thousands of protesting Americans during the late 1960s.

---

[16] Kunen, *The Strawberry Statement*, pp. 77, 78, 71–72.

6

AN ASSESSMENT

This study has selected, and attempted to indicate the nature of, successive and conflicting patterns of social thought: the early twentieth-century reform and radical progressive and pragmatic pattern; the succeeding pattern which was crystallized by the idea of European totalitarianism in the 1930s and which developed into the conservatism of the postwar era; the new radicalism and bohemianism of the 1960s and 1970s which has constituted a minority protest against the reigning intellectual temper.

What can be learned from this survey of the social thought of American intellectuals in the twentieth century? In what sense is knowledge of the past useful? Is one who lives in the present, with this knowledge of the past, any better able to understand the current debate over public policy? On the basis of this history, can one judge who was right or wrong in the past, and ascertain the proper social thought for the present?

The most obvious contribution of this history to the present is its demonstration that contemporary social thought has a historical dimension. Neither the dominant conservatism nor the challenging radicalism can be fully understood without an understanding of their past. This is to claim no more than what historical scholarship customarily tries to do. Most historians conceive their major job to be to describe, and in some sense to explain, their particular subject or time period in the past, and to indicate its relevance to other subjects or time periods. In the case of recent history, there may be a relevance not only to other subjects or time periods in the past, but to the present as well.

Granting that today's controversies in social thought are better understood with knowledge of their historical background, is there no further relevance of the past to the present? In order to answer this question, a word must be said concerning the influence of the intellectuals whose social thought has been discussed. This book obviously takes intellectuals and their ideas seriously. But their influence upon public policy is easily exaggerated, particularly by intellectuals themselves. The general statement can be made that intellectuals have contributed to the making of public policy in modern America in inverse relation to their estrangement at any particular time. When estranged as literary bohemians in the 1920s or political radicals in the 1930s, the intellectuals made little direct impact upon public policy. When they no longer expressed alienation, during the 1940s and 1950s, their social thought seems to have directly contributed to public policy. This is to admit, however, that the influence of the intellectuals is severely circumscribed. If they agree with current domestic or foreign policy, they appear to contribute to it through their support; if they disagree with current policy, they are ignored. The logic suggests inescapably that at all times the direct influence of intellectuals upon public policy is slight.

It is difficult of course to ascertain relative influence with precision. What influence the intellectuals do exercise is indirect, and stems from the overall climate of opinion which they have helped to create. The case of the radicals during the Depression is typical. The most that can be said for the impact of radicals upon Rooseveltian policy is that they defined an outer limit of alternative policy and criticism on the Left. They thus formed part of the whole context in which the New Deal occurred. Though there is no evidence that radicals directly influenced FDR, it is impossible to know whether he would have created the welfare state, to the extent that he did, if the Old Left had been absent.

If the intellectuals' relation to power, at most, has been indirect, their influence upon the creation of new life-styles has been direct and decisive. This is because, unlike the case of public policy decision making, innovation in styles of life occurs mainly among intellectuals, loosely defined. What this overall evaluation of intellectuals and their influence on the American scene probably means for the 1970s is that the significance of the radical social thought of intellectuals will be dual and separable. First,

New Left political radicalism will probably have no direct ascertainable influence upon public policy, but will mark outer limits of possible alternatives, as the Old Left did in the Depression. Whether the function of these radical alternatives will be to attract or to repel the major political currents is impossible to say. Second, the direct influence of radical lifestyle experimentation will likely continue among affluent younger Americans, particularly around college campuses. Such a future would, at least, be consistent with the past.

Can one make a judgment of social thought in the past, and in turn appraise what is wise or foolish in the present? The answer is a mixture of yes and no. An assessment of the profundity of ideas concerning society in the past cannot, strictly speaking, be made on the basis of knowledge of the ideas by themselves. Reference has to be made to the social realities to which the ideas originally referred. William Henry Chamberlin's sympathetic progressive and pragmatic interpretation of the Soviet Union in the 1920s, for instance, cannot be judged apart from an evaluation of conditions in the Soviet Union. The historian of social thought may or may not extend his investigation beyond ideas to the external realities. Sometimes, as in the case of Chamberlin's view that Soviet dictatorship would soon disappear, there is a clear consensus among American historians of the Soviet Union that his thought was wrong. It is ordinarily not so easy to judge social thought, even when it is in the past. Consider the question of how domestic radical thought in the 1930s should be appraised. Were the radicals right when they criticized Franklin Roosevelt for not trying to develop a systematically socialistic plan for the American economy? Were defenders of the New Deal right when they credited FDR with saving the country from revolution? Such questions require, among other things, assumptions or conclusions with regard to matters of fact. Would socialism have been accepted by the American people, and if accepted, would it have been economically superior? Would a revolution have occurred if there had been no New Deal? The answers to these questions are impossible to find. Yet evaluations of social thought must, in a strict sense, be tentative without answers to these questions.

A related problem is that the patterns of thought in the present may be the same as those in the past, but the facts to which they refer may be different. Thus, as was discussed in the case of C. Wright Mills's progressive and pragmatic interpretation of Castro's Cuban revolution (an interpretation which paralleled the Old Left's view of the Soviet revolutionary dictatorship during the 1920s and 1930s), one cannot with certainty, on the basis of the parallel in ideas alone, appraise Mills's thought as equally erroneous. One must ask whether the facts of Castro's Cuba equal the facts of Stalin's Russia. But it is even more difficult to reach a consensus concerning the facts in contemporary controversial events than to achieve a consensus on events in the past.

Tentative judgments therefore can be made, but of necessity they are frequently at best historically educated guesses. The major contribution of the historian to the present remains his sketch of the historical dimension of something in the present. This suggests that the aim of historical study ought to be detachment from, rather than involvement with, the partisan polemics of yesterday or today. In a time of crisis and commitment like the 1970s this is not a popular position to take. Both the Left and Right want historical scholarship to take sides. Not to do so is to invite the charge of indifference to pressing public issues, of the irrelevance of scholarship to morality. But the fundamental task of historical scholarship is not to assume intentionally partisan commitment and merely to add to the contemporary debate. It is, most broadly phrased, to attempt to increase our understanding of human behavior in the past, or more specifically in the case of the historian of social thought, to increase our understanding of intellectual behavior in the past. Detachment, in order that one's understanding of rival arguments be as full as possible, rather than partisan commitment to one argument or another, is the desired (if difficult to attain) perspective. A detached scholarly quest for understanding the past is the historian's only special contribution. He is no more moral, intelligent, prescient, or wise than other men. If he writes intentionally polemical history, history which is consciously committed to one side or another, he will be like any other polemicist. His detached attempt to understand human behavior in the past can, however, result in increasing our understanding of human behavior in the present. If we are to be wise in the present, as well as to be morally attuned, we need to know as much as we can about human behavior. There is no logical or otherwise necessary reason why to know more about the human condition is to be less sensitive to moral questions. Further, it is possible that increased knowledge of human behavior through detached scholarship will lead to moral formulations in the future which will not be limited by the partisan polemics of yesterday and today. But only through an initially detached perspective can such a moral transcendence occur.

Similarly, only through scholarly detachment can judgments of the past—admitting their necessary modesty and tentativeness—escape the earlier polemics. This study has suggested, for example, that there were weaknesses in both the early twentieth-century progressive and pragmatic mentality and that of the mid-century conservatism. The progressive reform mind was overly optimistic about the course of history, and the interwar radicals were as a result recklessly willing to defend revolutionary barbarisms in the name of progressive ends. Critical of traditional

American practices because they failed to match American ideals, the Old Left inconsistently excused Communist practices because of their high ideals. But a detached historical perspective can also see weaknesses in the conservatism which accompanied the discovery of totalitarianism, equally understandable in terms of its pattern of thought, but weaknesses nevertheless. The perception of totalitarianism as a style of governmental and social organization which subjugated the individual to the aims of the State was a profound and devastating one, particularly to former sympathizers of the European revolutionary dictatorships. But by failing to extend its critical analysis of the regimentation of government and society in Europe to all modern countries, including the United States, and by dividing the world into the totalitarian "others" and the free "us," mid-century conservative social thought contributed to a dulling of sensitivity concerning domestic American problems. A highly moral preoccupation with the sins of European revolutionary dictatorships came to be accompanied by a lessening of concern with the sins of American society. Attention paid racial persecution in Germany and peasant suffering in Russia came to be coupled with a lack of preoccupation with America's racially oppressed and economically impoverished. A wiser sense of the complexity of life on the part of the conservative mind of the time was joined by a failure to act resolutely on social problems which needed attention.

These judgments cut across the polemical lines of the past and, to some extent, of the present. After a detached study of social thought in the past, one's judgments may well point to the need for a reconstructed future. Precisely because one has historical knowledge, he may have a more acute sense of arguments offered in the present which are in fact historical. He may be able to spot ossified attachments to old patterns of thought. This study may indeed suggest that neither the early twentieth-century progressive-pragmatic temper nor the postwar conservative mind ought to command one's allegiance in the 1970s. The conservative's sense of the irony and tragedy in human history needs to be joined with the reformer's and radical's sense of moral urgency in dealing with the present. Perhaps an awareness of the historical dimension of current debates in social thought can provide a deeper understanding of them, and also free us from them.

SUGGESTIONS FOR
FURTHER READING

For those readers who would explore further the ideas and the people presented in this book, as well as their times and intellectual contemporaries, I recommend the following. Wherever they are available, I have indicated paperback editions of the works suggested.

CHAPTER 2

Conservative Social Darwinism and Reform Darwinism are explained in Richard Hofstadter, *Social Darwinism in American Thought* (Philadelphia, 1944), available in Beacon paperback; and Eric Goldman, *Rendezvous with Destiny* (New York, 1952), available in Vintage paperback. For an important article that points out certain limits in the influence of Social Darwinism upon businessmen, see Irvin G. Wyllie, "Social Darwinism and the Businessman," *Proceedings of the American Philosophical Society* 103 (October 1959):629–635.

The idea of Self-Help is traced in Irvin Wyllie, *The Self-Made Man in America* (New Brunswick, N.J., 1954), available in Free Press paperback; and John Cawelti, *Apostles of the Self-Made Man* (Chicago, 1965), available in Chicago paperback.

For the general background of progressive history, see Richard Hofstadter, *The Progressive Historians* (New York, 1968), available in

125

Vintage paperback; John Higham *et al., History* (Englewood Cliffs, N.J., 1965), pp. 104–131, 171–211, available in Prentice-Hall paperback; and R. A. Skotheim, *American Intellectual Histories and Historians* (Princeton, N.J., 1966), pp. 66–72, available in Princeton paperback.

The early Lippmann is studied thoughtfully in Charles Forcey, *The Crossroads of Liberalism* (New York, 1961), *passim*, available in Oxford paperback, and routinely by Edward and Frederick Schapsmeier in *Walter Lippmann: Philosopher-Journalist* (Washington, D.C., 1969), which covers his whole career. A collection of essays that ranges widely over Lippmann's thought is Marquis Childs and James Reston, eds., *Walter Lippmann and His Times* (Freeport, N.Y., 1959). Included is Arthur Schlesinger's good essay, "Walter Lippmann: The Intellectual v. Politics," pp. 189–225.

The nature and significance of the reformers' faith in progress, their pragmatic method, and their moral relativism combined with absolutism are variously analyzed by Eric Goldman, *Rendezvous with Destiny*; Morton White, *Social Thought in America: The Revolt against Formalism* (New York, 1949), available in Beacon paperback; David Noble, *The Paradox of Progressive Thought* (Minneapolis, 1958), available in Minnesota paperback; and Henry May, *The End of American Innocence* (New York, 1959), available in Quadrangle paperback.

The estrangement of the intellectuals before World War I is studied most comprehensively by Henry May in *The End of American Innocence*. Daniel Aaron investigates the political radicalism of alienated literary intellectuals between the wars in *Writers on the Left* (New York, 1961), as does James Gilbert in *Writers and Partisans* (New York, 1968). The life-style preoccupations, as well as other concerns, of estranged intellectuals before and after World War I can be explored through the published memoirs of participants, such as those by Hutchins Hapgood, Mabel Dodge Luhan, Sherwood Anderson, Floyd Dell, Emma Goldman, Susan Glaspell, Max Eastman, Conrad Aiken, Theodore Dreiser, Harriet Monroe, Ludwig Lewisohn, John Gould Fletcher, William Carlos Williams, Van Wyck Brooks, Matthew Josephson, Harold Stearns, Joseph Wood Krutch, and Malcolm Cowley. Of these memoirs, only Cowley's *Exile's Return* (New York, 1934), Viking Compass, and Hutchins Hapgood, *A Victorian in the Modern World* (Seattle, 1971), are available in paperback. Greenwich Village after the war is studied in Caroline Ware, *Greenwich Village, 1920–1930* (Boston, 1935). The meaning of the postwar French expatriation experience for American intellectuals is probed in Warren Susman, "A Second Country: The Expatriate Image," *Texas Studies in Literature and Language* 3 (Summer 1961):171–183.

Early American interpretations of European revolutionary dictatorships are studied in Christopher Lasch, *American Liberals and the Russian Revolution* (New York, 1962); Peter Filene, *Americans and the*

Soviet Experiment, 1917–1933 (Cambridge, Mass., 1967); and John Diggins, "Flirtation with Fascism: American Pragmatic Liberals and Mussolini's Italy," *American Historical Review* 71 (January 1966):487–506. Especially valuable will be Diggins's forthcoming book on the American response to Fascist Italy.

CHAPTER 3

The only survey of intellectual history in the Depression is Charles Alexander, *Nationalism in American Thought, 1930–1945* (New York, 1969), available in Rand McNally paperback. This volume has an excellent bibliography.

Intellectuals on the Left during the Depression are discussed by Frank Warren, *Liberals and Communism* (Bloomington, Ind., 1966); James Gilbert, *Writers and Partisans*; Irving Howe and Lewis Coser, *The American Communist Party* (Boston, 1957), pp. 273–318, available in Praeger paperback; Daniel Bell, *Marxian Socialism in the United States* (Princeton, N.J., 1967), pp. 134–193, available in Princeton paperback (originally published in Donald Egbert and Stow Persons, eds., *Socialism and American Life*, 2 vols. [Princeton, N.J., 1952]); as well as by Daniel Aaron, *Writers on the Left*, pp. 149–396.

Some of the memoirs by the intellectuals named above for the years before and after World War I carry their accounts into the 1930s. In addition, see Granville Hicks, *Where We Came Out* (New York, 1954), and *Part of the Truth: An Autobiography* (New York, 1965); Malcolm Cowley, *Think Back On Us*, ed. by Henry Dan Piper (Carbondale, Ill., 1967); and Alfred Kazin, *Starting Out in the Thirties* (Boston, 1965), available in Atlantic-Little, Brown paperback.

There were some intellectuals who, as exceptions to the critical generalization offered at the end of Chapter 3, did extend their discovery of totalitarianism to modern societies in general. See Erich Fromm, *Escape from Freedom* (New York, 1941), available in Avon paperback; for another critique which was offered later and which became important to the New Left in the 1960s, see Herbert Marcuse, *One-Dimensional Man* (Boston, 1964), available in Beacon paperback.

CHAPTER 4

There is little scholarship on the history of social thought in the 1930s; there is less on the postwar years. Even more than for the earlier period, one must turn to the writings of the leading intellectuals of the time. See, for various expressions of the "conservative" ideas of the forties and fifties, Reinhold Niebuhr, *The Children of Light and the Children of Darkness* (New York, 1944), available in Scribner paperback; Niebuhr, *The Irony of American History* (New York, 1952), available in Scribner paperback; Arthur Schlesinger, Jr., *The Vital Center* (Boston, 1949), available in Houghton Mifflin paperback; Joseph Wood Krutch, *The Measure of Man* (New York, 1954), available in Grosset & Dunlap paperback; Peter Viereck, *Conservatism Revisited* (New York, 1949), available in Free Press paperback as *Conservatism Revisited and the New Conservatism: What Went Wrong?*; Viereck, *Shame and Glory of the Intellectuals* (New York, 1953), available in revised Capricorn paperback; Daniel Bell, *The End of Ideology* (New York, 1960), available in Free Press paperback; Clinton Rossiter, *Conservatism in America* (New York, 1955), available in Vintage paperback; Russell Kirk, *The Conservative Mind* (Chicago, 1953), available in Regnery paperback; and William Buckley, *Up from Liberalism* (New York, 1959), available in Bantam paperback. Though the authors of these books, along with the figures discussed in the text, in common expressed a rejection of earlier progressive and pragmatic thought, they also vehemently disagreed on many public policy issues.

Historical scholarship in the 1940s and 1950s is discussed in John Higham *et al.*, *History*, pp. 132–144, 212–232, available in Prentice-Hall paperback; Richard Hofstadter, *The Progressive Historians*, pp. 437–466; Gene Wise, "Political 'Reality' in Recent American Scholarship: Progressives versus Symbolists," *American Quarterly* 19, pt. 2 (Summer 1967):303–328; and Wise, "Implicit Irony in Perry Miller's *New England Mind*," *Journal of the History of Ideas* 29 (October–December 1968):579–600.

A bibliography of the writings of Sidney Hook appears in John Kurtz, ed., *Sidney Hook and the Contemporary World* (New York, 1968), pp. 429–471.

CHAPTER 5

For examples of others on the Left, like C. Wright Mills, who were critical of the dominant currents of social thought in the 1950s, see Irving Howe, *Steady Work* (New York, 1966), available in Harvest paperback; and I. F. Stone, *The Haunted Fifties* (New York, 1963) available in Vintage paperback. For writings of intellectuals in the 1950s that have been significant as background for the preoccupation with new life-styles in the 1960s and 1970s, see Norman Mailer, *The White Negro* (San Francisco, 1957), available in City Lights paperback; Paul Goodman, *Growing Up Absurd* (New York, 1960), available in Vintage paperback; Herbert Marcuse, *Eros and Civilization* (Boston, 1955), available in Vintage paperback; Norman O. Brown, *Life against Death* (Middletown, Conn., 1959), available in Modern Library paperback; Brown, *Love's Body* (New York, 1966), available in Vintage paperback; and Allen

Ginsberg, *Empty Mirror* (New York, 1961), available in Corinth paperback.

A collection of New Left historical essays is in Barton Bernstein, ed., *Towards a New Past* (New York, 1967), available in Pantheon paperback. Selections from two New Left historians, and a review essay of New Left scholarship, appear in R. A. Skotheim, ed., *The Historian and the Climate of Opinion* (Reading, Mass., 1969), pp. 105–163, available in Addison-Wesley paperback. For the work of an important radical historian who has vigorously criticized the position expressed by Staughton Lynd, which is essentially that of Howard Zinn, see Eugene Genovese, *The Political Economy of Slavery* (New York, 1965), available in Pantheon paperback, and *The World the Slaveholders Made* (New York, 1969). The most recent sympathetic survey of New Left historical scholarship is a collaborative essay, "New Left Historians of the 1960s." *Radical America* 4 (November 1970):81–106.

Writings by and about the young political and life-style radicals are numerous and increasing daily. The more important early analyses include Kenneth Keniston, *The Uncommitted* (New York, 1965), available in Dell paperback; Keniston, *Young Radicals* (New York, 1968), available in Harvest paperback; Ronald Berman, *America in the Sixties* (New York, 1968), available in Harper paperback; Theodore Roszak, *The Making of a Counter Culture* (New York, 1969), available in Anchor paperback; Jack Newfield, *A Prophetic Minority* (New York, 1966), available in Signet paperback; and Paul Jacobs and Saul Landau, eds., *The New Radicals* (New York, 1966), available in Vintage paperback.

For a particularly provocative discussion of the role of the intellectual in modern America, which explores many of the themes of this book, see Christopher Lasch, *The New Radicalism in America* (New York, 1965), available in Vintage paperback.

Index

Acheson, Dean, 76
Adams, John, 74
Anderson, Sherwood, 6
Atlantic Charter, 72

Beard, Charles, 7, 16, 88, 89
Becker, Carl, 6, 7–8, 16
Bell, Daniel, 10
Bohemianism, *see* Life styles, new
Boorstin, Daniel, 90, 92
Brandeis, Louis, 14
Burke, Edmund, 74, 75
Burkhardt, Jacob, 74

Calhoun, John C., 74
Calverton, V. F., 6
Carnegie, Andrew, 12, 113
Castro, Fidel, 100–103
Central Intelligence Agency, 77
Chamberlin, William Henry: background,
  31–32; conservative thought, 41–44, 74–
  75; on Fascism, 42–43; on isolationism,
  43–44; on Soviet Union, 32–34, 40–42,
  70–75, 122

Chambers, Clarke, 38
Chambers, Whittaker, 76
Christian Science Monitor, 32
Civil liberties, 41–42, 47, 56, 62
Cohen, Morris, 45*n*
Cold War, 8, 72–75, 78, 82, 85–87, 99–
  100
Columbia University, 16, 26, 59, 96, 116–
  118
Committee for Cultural Freedom, 5–6
Communism, international, *see* U.S.S.R.
Communist International, 72–73
Communist Party, American, 40, 77
Consensus interpretation of American his-
  tory, 90
Conservatism: in Boorstin, 90; in Cham-
  berlin, 41–44, 72–75; in Hofstadter, 91–
  93; in Hook, 51–52, 78–82; in Krutch,
  61–63; in Lippmann, 52–57, 82–85. *See
  also* Darwinism, Reembracement of
  America, Self–Help myth
Containment, 86–87
Cowley, Malcolm, 30–31

Croly, Herbert, 19
Cuba, 100–103

Daily Worker, The, 6
Darwin, Charles, 14
Darwinism: Conservative Social, 14; in James, William, 24; Reform, 14
Davis, Elmer, 6
Debs, Eugene, 15
Dewey, John, 3, 5, 16, 45n: on New Deal, 39; on pragmatism and reform, 26–29; on Soviet Union, 28–29
Dictatorships, *see* U.S.S.R., Fascism
Disney, Walt, 118
Dos Passos, John, 6, 7
Duranty, Walter, 32

Eastman, Max, 6
Eddy, Sherwood, 45n
Estrangement of the intellectuals, 30–31, 104–105, 121. *See also* Intellectuals
Experimental method, 2–4; in Chamberlin, 32–33; in Dewey, 26–29; in Hook, 50–51, 78–79; in James, 24–26; in Lippmann, 20–23; in Mills, 100–102; in Robinson, 16–18; in Steffens, 35–37; in Zinn, 110–112. *See also* Pragmatism

Fascism, 5, 35–36, 42–43, 48, 56, 64, 68–69
Fifth Amendment, 81
Fischer, Louis, 32
Five Year Plan, 40–41
Franco, 8
Frank, Waldo, 6
Frankfurter, Felix, 76
Franklin, Benjamin, 13
Fuchs, Klaus, 76

Godkin lectures, 52–53
Gold, Harry, 76–77
Government Operations Committee, 77
Greenglass, David, 76–77
Guttmann, Allen, 74–75

Hartz, Louis, 26, 90, 92
Heller, Joseph, 116
Hicks, Granville, 6
Higham, John, 89
Hiss, Alger, 76
Hitler, *see* Fascism

Hofstadter, Richard, 87–93
Holmes, Oliver Wendell, 14
Hook, Sidney, 5; background, 45; on Cold War, 79–82; conservative thought, 51–52, 78–82; on democracy, 49–50; on experimental method, 50–51, 78–79; on Fascism, 48; on Marx, 45–46; on McCarthyism, 81–82; reembracement of America, 49–51; on Soviet Union, 46–47; on violence, 46–47
Horatio Alger myth, *see* Self–Help myth
Horowitz, Irving Louis, 106n
Hutchins, Robert, 81

Instrumentalism, *see* Pragmatism
Intellectuals: estrangement from America, 30–31; influence in society, 121–122; on New Deal, 39–40; reembracement of America, 7–8, 66–67, 78, 94–95
Internal Security Act, 77
Intervention in World War II, 57–58, 65

James, William, 3, 24–26
Josephson, Matthew, 6

Kallen, Horace, 5
Kennan, George, 86–87
Kennedy, Gail, 25n
Krutch, Joseph Wood: background, 59; conservative thought, 61–63; on esthetics, 61–62; on Europe, 62–68; on radicalism, 63; on science, 60; on Soviet Union, 60–61; on totalitarianism, 63
Kunen, James Simon: on Columbia demonstrations, 117–118; on Vietnam, 119

Lamont, Corliss, 6
Lasch, Christopher, 35
Lerner, Max, 6, 50
Lewis, Sinclair, 6, 7
Life magazine, 58
Life styles, new, 30–31, 112–116, 121–122
Lippmann, Walter: on Cold War, 85–87; on collectivism, 53–54; on democracy, 20–21, 22, 83–84; on intervention, 57–58; on liberalism, 56–57; compared with Mills, 97; on the press, 21; reembracement of America, 52–58; on scientific method, 20, 22–23; on traditional values, 52–53, 83–85

Lundberg, Ferdinand, 5
Lyons, Eugene, 5, 6

Marxism, 45
Mather, Cotton, 13
McCarthy, Joseph, 74
McCarthyism, 75–77, 81–82
McGiffert, Michael, 13n
Mills, C. Wright: on American democracy, 98–99; on American totalitarianism, 97–99; background, 96; on Cold War, 99–100; on Cuba, 100–103, 122–123; on European totalitarianism, 97; on intellectuals, 103–105; on Soviet Union, 99–100
Mussolini, 35–36
Myers, Gustavus, 35

Nation, The, 6, 59, 61–62
Nazi–Soviet nonaggression pact, 6, 50, 65, 69
New Deal, 39, 44, 52, 53–56, 80, 91
New Left, see Radical thought, Kunen, Mills, Zinn
New Republic, 19, 69
Nixon, Richard, 76
Nonintervention in World War II, 43–44

Odets, Clifford, 6
Old Left, see Radical thought, Chamberlin, Hook, Steffens

Parrington, Vernon Louis, 16
Perry, Ralph Barton, 24n, 13n, 25n
Phillips, David Graham, 35
Popular Front, 40
Populism, 91–92
Pound, Roscoe, 14
Pragmatism, 2–4, 23–29, 45–46, 79, 102, 111–112. See also Experimental method
Progress, belief in: in Chamberlin, 33–34; in James, 26; in Mills, 101; in Robinson, 17–19; in Steffens, 36–37; in Zinn, 110–111
Progressive historians, 16–19, 89, 106–107. See also James Harvey Robinson
Progressivism, 2–4, 14–15, 18, 29–30, 91–92. See also Dewey, James, Lippmann, Robinson

Radical thought: New Left, 8–10, 94–96, 107, 124; Old Left, 3–10, 29–30, 39–40. See also Chamberlin, Hook, Kunen, Mills, Steffens, Zinn
Reembracement of America, 7–8, 66–67, 124; by Chamberlin, 43; by Hook, 49–51; by Lippmann, 52–58
Reform thought, 2–4, 29–30, 36, 38–39, 91–92. See also Dewey, James, Lippmann, Robinson
Reinitz, Richard, 66–67
Robinson, James Harvey, 16–19
Rockefeller, John D., 12
Roosevelt, Franklin, 38–39, 71–72, 74, 107, 122
Roosevelt, Theodore, 15
Rosenberg, Julius and Ethel, 77
Russell, Bertrand, 45n
Russia, see U.S.S.R.

Salinger, J. D., 116
Saturday Evening Post, 69
Schuman, Frederick, 6
Scientific method, see Experimental method
Self–Help myth, 13–14, 75, 95, 113–116
Sheean, Vincent, 6
Sinclair, Upton, 35
Skotheim, Robert Allen, 1n
Stalin, Joseph, 70–71. See also U.S.S.R.
Stearns, Harold, 30
Steffens, Lincoln, 35–37
Stevenson, Adlai, 76
Stone, I. F., 6
Subversive Activities Control Board, 77

Taft, William Howard, 15
Tarbell, Ida, 35
Thomas, Norman, 6
Thurber, James, 6
Tocqueville, Alexis de, 74, 90
Totalitarianism, American: in Mills, 97–99; interpreted by New Left, 8–9; European: in Chamberlin, 43, 65, 71; in Hofstadter, 92; in Hook, 50–52, 65, 78–82; in Krutch, 63, 65; in Lippmann, 52–58, 65; in Mills, 97; interpreted by Old Left, 1–8, 65–66, 88–89
Turner, Frederick Jackson, 16
Tydings, Millard, 77

U.S.S.R.: in Chamberlin, 32–34, 40–42, 70–73; in Dewey, 28–29; and Fascism, 64–65; in Hook, 46–47, 79–82; in Krutch, 60–61; in *Life*, 69; in Lippmann, 55–56, 85–87; in Mills, 99–100; in *New Republic*, 69; in *Saturday Evening Post*, 69; viewed by New Left, 8; viewed by Old Left, 4, 5–7, 44

Vietnam, 112, 117–119
Villard, Oswald Garrison, 6
Violence: in Hook, 46–47; in Mills, 101; viewed by New Left, 9; viewed by Old Left, 3, 4
Voice of America, 77

Weyl, Walter, 19
Wiebe, Robert, 12
Williams, William Carlos, 6
Wilson, Woodrow, 15, 19–20, 87
World War II, 57–58, 68–69, 71–72

Zinn, Howard: background, 111; as pragmatist, 111; on radical history, 110–111; on traditional history, 108–109